Cambridge English

Compact
First for Schools
Second Edition

Student's Book with answers

Barbara Thomas
Laura Matthews

Cambridge University Press
www.cambridge.org/elt

Cambridge Assessment English
www.cambridgeenglish.org

Information on this title: www.cambridge.org/9781107415607

© Cambridge University Press and UCLES 2014

This publication is in copyright. Subject to statutory exception
and to the provisions of relevant collective licensing agreements,
no reproduction of any part may take place without the written
permission of the publishers.

First published © Cambridge University Press and UCLES 2013

20 19 18

Printed in Poland by Opolgraf

A catalogue record for this publication is available from the British Library

ISBN 978-1-107-41556-0 Student's Book without answers with CD-ROM
ISBN 978-1-107-41560-7 Student's Book with answers with CD-ROM
ISBN 978-1-107-41567-6 Teacher's Book
ISBN 978-1-107-41577-5 Workbook without answers with Audio
ISBN 978-1-107-41572-0 Workbook with answers with Audio
ISBN 978-1-107-41558-4 Student's Pack (Student's Book without answers with CD-ROM and Workbook without answers with Audio)
ISBN 978-1-107-41574-4 Class Audio CD
ISBN 978-1-107-41604-8 Presentation Plus DVD-ROM

Additional resources for this publication at www.cambridge.org/compactfirstforschools2

The publishers have no responsibility for the persistence or accuracy of URLs
for external or third-party internet websites referred to in this publication, and
do not guarantee that any content on such websites is, or will remain, accurate
or appropriate. Information regarding prices, travel timetables, and other factual
information given in this work is correct at the time of first printing but the
publishers do not guarantee the accuracy of such information thereafter.

CONTENTS

	Map of the units	4
1	Family and friends	6
2	Exploring the world	14
3	The entertainment industry	22
4	Active life	30
5	Learning	38
6	Natural world	46
7	People and style	54
8	Keeping up to date	62
	Revision	70
	G Grammar reference	78
	W Writing guide	86
	Irregular verbs	93
	Wordlist	95
	Answer Key	103
	Acknowledgements	136

MAP OF THE UNITS

Unit	Topics	Grammar	Vocabulary	Writing
1 Family and friends	Family celebrations Friends	Present and future tenses State verbs Comparisons	Words often confused Matching expressions with similar meanings	Part 1: Essay understanding the question, paragraphing, linking words and phrases
2 Exploring the world	Adventure and travel Where you live	Past tenses Prepositions of time Adverb formation	Word building (1): adjective suffixes (-able, -al, -ous) Cities, towns and villages	Part 2: Story sequencing, using a range of past tenses, adjectives and adverbs
3 The entertainment industry	Films Music	Linking words and phrases The passive	Film and cinema Music	Part 2: Review organising paragraphs, recommending, using linking words and phrases
4 Active life	Sports Keeping fit and healthy	Modal verbs Prepositions following verbs and adjectives	Sports Food Word building (2): noun suffixes (-ence, -ity, -(s/t)ion)	Part 2: Letter and email giving advice, making suggestions, persuading, beginnings and endings
5 Learning	Ambitions and achievements Education	Conditionals	Phrasal verbs Careers Education	Part 2: Set text characters, events, types of question
6 Natural world	Environment and weather Wildlife	Countable and uncountable nouns Articles so and such (a/an), too and enough	Climate Environmental problems Animals	Part 2: Article keeping the reader's attention, describing and linking
7 People and style	Shopping and fashion People and feelings	Verbs and expressions followed by to-infinitive or -ing form Reported speech	Clothes Shopping Feelings	Part 2: Letter and email giving information, using linking words and phrases
8 Keeping up to date	Science Technology	Relative clauses	Science Computers Word building (3): prefixes and suffixes	Part 1: Essay planning, introductions and conclusions, using a range of vocabulary

Reading and Use of English		Listening	Speaking
Part 5: multiple-choice questions	Part 1: multiple-choice cloze	Part 3: multiple-matching	Part 1: leisure activities Part 2: comparing ways of spending free time
Part 6: gapped text	Part 2: open cloze Part 3: word formation	Part 1: multiple-choice questions + short recordings	Part 3: discussing preferences, agreeing and disagreeing Part 4: talking about where you live
Part 7: multiple-matching	Part 4: key word transformations	Part 4: multiple-choice questions + long recording	Part 1: adding extra information and comments Part 2: talking about films and music, avoiding unknown words, giving preferences
Part 5: multiple-choice questions	Part 2: open cloze Part 3: word formation	Part 2: sentence completion	Part 3: asking for opinions and reacting to opinions Part 4: discussing sports and keeping fit
Part 7: multiple-matching	Part 1: multiple-choice cloze Part 4: key word transformations	Part 2: sentence completion	Part 1: discussing ambitions, achievements and education Part 2: making guesses
Part 6: gapped text	Part 2: open cloze	Part 4: multiple-choice questions + long recording	Part 3: agreeing, disagreeing, making a comment or suggestion Part 4: discussing ways of helping the environment
Part 5: multiple-choice questions	Part 4: key word transformations	Part 3: multiple-matching	Part 1: expressing likes and dislikes Part 2: comparing different ways of shopping
Part 7: multiple-matching	Part 3: word formation	Part 1: multiple-choice questions + short recordings	Part 3: structuring a conversation Part 4: discussing technology

Family and friends
LISTENING

Part 3

1 Look at the photos, which all show families getting together. Is everybody enjoying themselves? Why do you think they are spending time together?

2 Work in pairs. Talk about family celebrations. What do you celebrate with your family? How do you celebrate? Which celebrations do you like best?

3 🔘 02 Listen to Emily talking about a family celebration. Answer these questions.

1 What usually happens? Is it usually well organised?
2 Was there a change of plan this year? Did everything go well?
3 Did anyone disagree with the plan?

4 🔘 02 Listen again. What does Emily say about her family's celebration? Choose one answer from A–F. Your answers in Exercise 3 will help you.

A It was less well organised than usual.
B There was an unexpected event on the day.
C It lasted longer than usual.
D There was a difference of opinion.
E A change of plan was successful.
F The day started off badly.

> **Exam tip**
>
> A statement may refer to a particular part of what the speaker says or it may refer to what the speaker says as a whole. You need to listen both for details and for general meaning.

Exam task

The task below is shorter than in the exam. In Listening Part 3 you hear five speakers and you select the correct answer from a choice of eight possible statements. You have already heard Emily. Now you will hear three more people.

🔘 03 You will hear three people talking about a family celebration. Choose from the list A–F what each speaker says about the celebration.

A It was less well organised than usual.
B There was an unexpected event on the day.
C It lasted longer than usual.
D There was a difference of opinion.
E A change of plan was successful.
F The day started off badly.

Speaker 1 .....
Speaker 2 .....
Speaker 3 .....

> **Exam tip**
>
> In the exam, you will hear each recording twice, so don't worry if you don't get all the answers the first time.

READING AND USE OF ENGLISH

Part 1

Vocabulary – Words often confused

1 👁 Work in pairs. Complete the sentences with the correct word or expression.

> **Exam tip**
>
> This part of the exam tests mainly vocabulary but some questions will test grammar too.

1 Here are some fixed expressions with *at*. Check the meaning of each phrase in each gap and then choose the correct expression.

| at all   at last   at least   at once |

  A Most of my friends have .... one computer in their homes.
  B I got into bed and I was so tired I fell asleep ....
  C I waited for my friend for ages and .... she arrived.
  D She didn't know her grandfather .... because he never visited.

2 Sometimes you need to look at the meaning of the word and also the grammar. Choose the correct word for each gap.

| believes   demands   depends   expects |

  A Our teacher .... us to speak English in her lessons.
  B Playing chess .... a lot of concentration.
  C My granny .... on us to get all her shopping for her.
  D My father .... in letting me make my own decisions.

2 Quickly read the text in the Exam task. Answer these questions.

  1 What is significant about 21 December in the most northern / most southern places?
  2 What do people celebrate in northern countries in the middle of December?

Exam task

For questions **1–8**, read the text below and decide which answer (A, B, C or D) best fits each gap. There is an example at the beginning (0).

Winter celebrations

In the countries which are furthest north and south on Earth, the **(0)** ..A.. of light varies hugely between winter and summer. In the northern hemisphere, the shortest day is on or about 21 December. In **(1)** .... fact, in some places there is no daylight at **(2)** .... during the day in the middle of winter. In the southern hemisphere, 21 December is the longest day, of course.

Throughout history, people in **(3)** .... every northern country have **(4)** .... traditions to celebrate the fact that the days would **(5)** .... both lighter and longer after the middle of December. From then onwards, people would wait impatiently for the return of the sun, which they **(6)** .... on. They were hunters, so the seasons and the weather **(7)** .... a very important part in their lives. Food was in short supply in winter months, so a whole community would share meals. They lit fires and candles and sang and danced. Some of the traditions **(8)** .... to this day.

0	**A** amount	**B** number	**C** total	**D** size
1	**A** genuine	**B** actual	**C** true	**D** real
2	**A** least	**B** once	**C** last	**D** all
3	**A** about	**B** virtually	**C** approximately	**D** quite
4	**A** expanded	**B** advanced	**C** progressed	**D** developed
5	**A** increase	**B** happen	**C** get	**D** change
6	**A** depended	**B** demanded	**C** believed	**D** expected
7	**A** made	**B** played	**C** produced	**D** involved
8	**A** survive	**B** support	**C** keep	**D** maintain

3 Read the text again and check your answers. Does each one fit the meaning?

READING AND USE OF ENGLISH   UNIT 1   7

1 SPEAKING

Part 1

Friends

1 **04** Look at the Speaking Part 1 questions and the possible answers in the table below. Listen to George and Francesca answering the questions. Note down the extra information they add.

Question	Answer	Extra information
1 Do you do any activities after school?	diving	
2 When do you do your homework?	after dinner	
3 What do you usually do at the weekend?	meet friends, see grandmother	
4 What are you going to do next weekend?	friends, cinema, guitar	

2 **04** Complete these sentences from the recording. Listen again if you need to.

1 I .... to dive.
2 When I .... home from school, I .... TV.
3 On Saturday I .... the bus to town.
4 We .... to the cinema.
5 I .... my guitar most of the day.
6 I .... in a concert next Tuesday.

Grammar – Present and future tenses G *See page 78*

3 Work in pairs. Look at the tenses George and Francesca use to talk about the present and future.

1 Which tense does George use when he talks about diving?
2 Which tense does he use for the things he does regularly?
3 Francesca uses two different tenses to talk about next Saturday. Why?
4 Why does she use a continuous tense to talk about playing the guitar on Sunday?
5 Which tense does she use to talk about the concert? Is it definitely happening?

4 Look at the sentences in A and B below. Which is correct, A or B?

A	B
I like to relax.	I'm liking to relax.
I prefer to do my homework after dinner.	I'm preferring to do my homework after dinner.
I know I need to practise.	I'm knowing I need to practise.

What do you notice about the verbs *like*, *prefer* and *know*? Can you think of other verbs which behave in the same way?

5 ⊙ Choose the correct answer.

1 Amy, can I change the time that we *meet / 're meeting* tomorrow?
2 I *want / 'm wanting* to visit you soon.
3 I *normally spend / 'm normally spending* most of July at the seaside.
4 Next Saturday we *go / 're going* to a Greek restaurant.
5 I *'m thinking / think* it is a good idea to go camping.
6 We will be very tired when we *get / 'll get* home.
7 Tomorrow I can't come to school because I *'ll go / 'm going* to the dentist.
8 I'll do my homework in the morning before I *'ll go / go* to school.
9 I *write / 'm writing* this note to tell you that I *miss / 'm going to miss* tomorrow's class.
10 I'm really happy that you *come / 're coming* to Italy.

Exam task

Now work with a partner and ask and answer the questions in Exercise 1.

> **Exam tip**
>
> You will get more marks if you add some detail. To expand your answers think about why, when and how you do things.

Part 2

6 Look at the first two photographs. Which of the following adjectives, verbs, nouns and expressions could you use to talk about them?

bored ☐   energetic ☐   crowded ☐
excited ☐   lazy ☐
chat ☐   concentrate ☐   relax ☐
countryside ☐   exercise ☐
in the distance ☐   indoors ☐   outdoors ☐
a quiet spot ☐   fresh air ☐   in the shade ☐

7 Think of the advantages of spending your time like the people in these two photographs.

🔊 **05** Listen to Francesca's answer. Does she give the same advantages as you?

Grammar – Comparisons **G** *See page 78*

9 These sentences make comparisons with different adjectives and nouns. Put the words in *italics* in the correct order.

1 The people in the first photograph *much / than / probably / are / happier* than the people in the second one.
2 They *less / than / will / money / spend* going to the gym.
3 The people in the second photo are indoors, which *enjoyable / being / as / isn't / as* in the fresh air.
4 They *getting / exercise / probably / more / are /*.
5 They *than / energetic / are / more / being* the people in the first photograph.

10 Look at the other two photos above. Write two or three sentences comparing them, using some of these words.

| expensive | far more | fun | interesting |
| much less | thrilling | | |

Exam task

Work in pairs. Choose two of the photographs each. Take turns to talk about your photographs and compare them. Time yourselves. Try to talk for about one minute each and answer this question.

- What are the advantages for the people of spending their free time in these ways?

Exam tip ›

The question you have to answer is printed above the photographs in the exam. Make sure you answer this question when you are talking.

When you have finished, ask your partner this question. In the exam you have about 30 seconds to answer.

Which of these things would you prefer to do with your friends? Why?

9

1 READING AND USE OF ENGLISH

Part 5

1 You are going to read an extract from a novel about three girls. Look at the picture and answer these questions with a partner.

   1 Where are the girls?
   2 Do you think they know each other well?
   3 One of them has some news. Do you think it's good news or bad news?

2 Read the text very quickly and answer these questions.

   1 What news does Sierra give Amy and Vicki? How does she feel about it?
   2 How does Amy feel about Sierra's news?
   3 What do they make plans for?

> **Exam tip**
>
> Before you answer the questions, always read the text quickly to get an idea of what it is about.

Exam task

In Reading and Use of English Part 5, there are always six multiple-choice questions about one text. The text below is shorter than in the exam and there are only four questions.

For questions 1–4 on page 11, choose the answer (A, B, C or D) which you think fits best according to the text.

Vicki swept past the tables to the counter. Watching her, Sierra thought about the contrast between her two friends. If Amy zigzagged through life with her head down, Vicki moved through her days at full speed, with her chin to the sky and the wind in her long, silky, brown hair. That zestful optimism eventually had linked Sierra and Vicki, even though Sierra originally had interpreted Vicki's bold approach to life as arrogance.

The instant Vicki returned to their table, Sierra spilled her news. "Okay, are you both ready for my big announcement?"

"It can't be that huge if you didn't tell me at lunch today and made me wait until now," Vicki said, carefully pouring her tea over the glass of crushed ice.

"I wanted to tell you both at the same time."

"I appreciate that," Amy said.

"So?" Vicki prompted.

"Last night my brother called and told me he's going to Southern California next week. He's pretty sure he wants to attend Rancho Corona University for his Master's degree, but he wanted to check out some colleges before he made a final decision."

"That's your big news?" Vicki asked. Her pretty face took on a teasing grin. "You definitely could have told me that at lunch."

"Wait," Sierra said, her enthusiasm unruffled. "He's going to drive down there next week, and he asked if I wanted to go with him, and my parents said yes!"   line 18

"Good for you," Vicki said. "Bring back something for each of us."

"Didn't you go to California last year for Easter vacation?" Amy asked.

"Yes."

"And you also flew down there for your friends' wedding last summer." Amy turned her lower lip into a friendly pout. "How do you expect us to be happy for you again? You keep going on these adventures, and we don't go anywhere. I've never been to California – ever – in my life. I've only been to Seattle – once."

"I hope you have a good time," Vicki said cheerfully to Sierra.

Sierra broke into a wide grin. "You mean you hope we have a good time."

"'We' meaning you and Wes?" Vicki ventured. "Or 'we' meaning the three of us?"

"All of us!" Sierra spouted. "My brother is driving my parents' van down, and they said I could invite my friends to go."

"When do we leave?" Vicki asked.

"Wednesday after school," Sierra said.

The three friends bent their heads close. They began to make a plan for their upcoming road trip as the spring sunshine lit their little corner of the world. Sierra felt a gleeful rush of anticipation and knew it couldn't come fast enough for her.

10 UNIT 1 READING AND USE OF ENGLISH

Before you decide on your answer to each question, read the tip above it to help you.

> Underline the words in the text which give you the answer to question 1.

1 What do we find out about Sierra's attitude towards her friends in the first paragraph?
   A She wishes Vicki and Amy were more similar to each other.
   B She feels more positively towards Vicki than she once did.
   C She always knew she and Vicki would be friends.
   D She thinks Amy has a better approach to life than Vicki.

> Find the part of the text where Amy is speaking and answer question 3.

3 How does Amy react to Sierra's news?
   A She thinks Sierra isn't grateful enough for the opportunities she has.
   B She doesn't understand why Sierra wants to go away so much.
   C She thinks it's strange that Sierra keeps going to the same places.
   D She feels jealous of the experiences which Sierra is able to have.

> Some questions ask you about a particular word or an expression. Find the answer by reading the part of the text before and after it very carefully. Find the answer to question 2.

2 The writer uses the expression 'her enthusiasm unruffled' in line 18 to show that Sierra
   A wasn't put off by the reaction she received.
   B felt annoyed that she was being hurried.
   C felt confused about how she should continue.
   D didn't understand why she had to explain.

> Some questions ask you what a word like *it* or *that* refers to. The answer may be in a different sentence or in the same sentence. Underline *plan*, *road trip*, *spring sunshine* and *rush of anticipation* in the last paragraph. Read the whole paragraph and decide which can replace *it* in the last sentence.

4 What couldn't come fast enough?
   A the plan
   B the road trip
   C the spring sunshine
   D the rush of anticipation

Vocabulary – Matching expressions with similar meanings

3 To answer multiple-choice questions you often need to find words in the text with a similar meaning to words in the options. Read the paragraph and think about what is happening. Underline the words which match the expressions below. Write the number of the phrase next to the part of the text it matches.

> Marcus stood and watched as Jake came through the school gate. He realised he couldn't trust Jake and now he wondered why he had always been so keen to get his approval. Jake was walking in a way that Marcus had never noticed before. He really thought he was better than the rest of them. He was heading now towards a couple of boys who were standing near Marcus. Marcus saw them look up. He realised Jake was asking one of them to do something. The boy looked very unsure and worried – it must have been something that wasn't allowed. The other boy relaxed, glad that it wasn't him who had been chosen. Marcus started to feel rather annoyed about the way Jake behaved. Why should he make that boy do something he didn't want to? Marcus suddenly made up his mind he would tackle Jake. He wasn't going to let him get away with it this time.

1 eager to please   2 was arrogant   3 doubtful about something
4 seemed relieved   5 irritated   6 decided   7 stand up to

1 WRITING

Part 1: Essay

"This is my new friend, Roger - he's a real down-to-earth kind of guy."

Work in pairs.

1 Describe your family. Which members of the family are most important to you? Why?

2 Talk about your friends. Do you have lots of friends, or just a few good ones? Where did you meet them?

3 Answer these questions. Write A for family and B for friends.

Who: takes care of you? ☐ gives you advice? ☐ teaches you to do things? ☐

Who do you: have most fun with? ☐ spend most time with? ☐ get on best with? ☐

Discuss your answers with your partner. Are your answers true just at a certain stage of your life (baby, young child, teenager) or for all ages?

4 Now read the exam task at the top of the next column and answer the true/false questions below with your partner.

True or false?

1 You have a choice of question in Part 1 of the Writing paper.
2 You must write an essay of at least 190 words.
3 The first sentence of the task helps you to understand what you must write about.
4 You are asked to compare two things in this essay.
5 You should write about teenagers in general, and not just yourself.
6 When you give 'your own idea' it should be different from points 1 and 2.

You **must** answer this question. Write your answer in **140–190 words** in an appropriate style on the separate answer sheet.

In your English class you have been talking about your family and friends. Now your English teacher has asked you to write an essay for homework.

Write your essay using **all** the notes and giving reasons for your point of view.

Which is more important to teenagers: their family or their friends?

Notes
Write about:
    1. who teenagers spend most time with
    2. who gives teenagers most support
    3. .... (your own idea)

5 Look back at the questions you answered in Exercise 3. Discuss with your partner whether you could write about anything here as 'your own idea' in point 3 of the essay. Put a tick next to anything you could use, and a cross next to anything you could not use.

6 Read the two answers to the exam question and then complete the chart and answer the questions below with your partner.

A

By the time they are about 14, teenagers probably spend more time with their friends than with their family. They are at school every day and therefore in the company of their friends. In addition, they play sport with these friends, go into town with them or go round to their houses at the weekend.

Yet all teenagers still rely heavily on their families, and their parents especially, for support and advice. Parents have more experience and more knowledge to share than friends, and they can help with important decisions about every aspect of your life as a teenager. They will also be on your side if you fall out with your friends, which unfortunately can happen!

In general though, I would say that most teenagers get on better with their friends than their families. They are the same age, so they share the same tastes in music and clothes and so on. They have very similar ideas too. As a result, parents are often much less important to their children at this stage.

Therefore, I personally think that for most teenagers, their friends are more important than their family.

UNIT 1 WRITING

B

I'm a teenager, and I spend a lot of time with my friends during term time, both at school and outside school. Of course I also spend time with my family, especially during the school holidays, but overall I spend slightly more time with my friends. I think that's true for most teenagers.

As for support, I am lucky that my family have always helped me. Yet my best friend also helps me a lot now if I have problems. This happens with many teenagers, that gradually they start asking their friends for help and advice as well as their family.

One day every teenager will leave home and start a life without their parents and family, but for most people their family is always part of their life. In contrast, some of the friends you make when you are very young get forgotten when you grow up and you make new friends.

For that reason, I think that for me, and for teenagers in general, family are in the end more important than friends.

Which is more important to teenagers: family or friends?	Essay A	Essay B
Main points	friends	
1 time		
2 support		
3 ?		
Conclusion		

Are the essays written in a formal or informal style?

Which is more important to you personally, family or friends? Underline the points of view in the answers which you agree with.

7 Find these linking expressions in essays A and B and underline them.

> as for   for that reason   in addition   in contrast
> in general   overall   therefore   yet

Now choose the correct linking expressions below.

I love going out with my friends but (1) *in addition / in general* the rest of my family aren't as sociable as me. (2) *As for / Yet* my grandparents, they're much happier at home. (3) *In other words / In fact*, they're always busy as they've got lots of hobbies. (4) *For that reason / For example*, I always ring them before I go there in case they're in the middle of doing something. (5) *Yet / Therefore* if I do just turn up, they don't mind. (6) *Nevertheless / In contrast*, my friend's grandparents are always going away so she hardly ever sees them.

8 Read the exam task and think about what you can write about in points 1 and 2. Write some notes. Then write down your idea for point 3, and what your conclusion will be.

When you have finished, discuss your ideas with a partner. Then do the task.

> **Exam tip**
>
> It is important to decide what you are going to say in your essay before you start writing. In the exam, you can write your plan on the exam paper.

Exam task

In your English class you have been talking about the part grandparents and older people play in young people's lives. Now your English teacher has asked you to write an essay for homework.

Write your essay using **all** the notes and giving reasons for your point of view.

> 'Young people learn a lot from their grandparents and other older people.'
> Do you agree?
>
> **Notes**
> Write about:
>
> 1. the past
> 2. technology
> 3. .... (your own idea)

> **Exam tip**
>
> When you have finished writing, read your essay carefully to check for grammar and spelling mistakes.

 See page 86

2 Exploring the world
READING AND USE OF ENGLISH

Adventure and travel

Part 6

1. Look at the young people in the photos. Work in pairs to answer the questions.
   1. What are the teenagers doing? Have you ever done any of these things?
   2. Do you think teenagers enjoy doing dangerous activities more than older people?

2. You are going to read about a boy called Parker who went to the North Pole. Look at the text. What does the title tell you?

3. Quickly read the text to understand what happened and answer the questions. Don't worry about the missing sentences.
   1. How far was the journey?
   2. Who went with Parker?
   3. What was the weather like?
   4. What problem did they have?

4. Complete gaps 1–6 with sentences A–F.

> ### He nearly reached the top of the world
>
> Few people have succeeded in skiing to the North Pole. (1) .... To do so, Parker had to cover 180 kilometres across snow and ice to reach his destination. (2) .... They had been accompanied by their parents but Parker was with just a guide called Doug. (3) .... During the journey they knew they would be faced with freezing wind and low temperatures. (4) .... Doug had experience of other problems too, like cracks opening up in the ice. (5) .... In fact, the gaps in the ice were much larger than they had expected because of global warming. (6) .... The gaps were just too wide for the two explorers to cross. So they had to give up* and Parker travelled the last 15 miles in a helicopter, having been defeated by his reason for the trip – global warming.
>
> *A year later Parker tried again and was successful.

A Two other teenagers had previously got there on skis but they had had a different starting point so had only gone half this distance.
B Teenager Parker Liautaud attempted to become one of them in order to draw attention to the effects of global warming.
C They have been known to reach –50°C in this part of the world.
D Parker had complete confidence in him because this would be his seventh trip.
E Doug hadn't seen anything as bad as that on his previous trips.
F These can appear faster than a man can walk and can become a real challenge.

5. Underline these words in the sentences A–F in Exercise 4 and say what each one refers to in the story.
   1. *there* (A) ....
   2. *them* (B) ....
   3. *they* (C) ....
   4. *him* and *his* (D) ....
   5. *that* (E) ....
   6. *these* (F) ....

Exam tip

When you decide which sentence goes in each gap, make sure *they*, *them* and *these* refer back to a plural noun and *he* and *him* to a singular noun. Then check the meaning fits too.

Exam task

In Reading Part 6 there are six gaps and seven sentences. The text below has four gaps and five sentences.

You are going to read a text written by a teenager about explorers. Four sentences have been removed from the text. Choose from the sentences A–E the one which fits each gap (1–4). There is one extra sentence which you do not need to use.

My future as an explorer

I've always wanted to be an explorer. When I was very small my favourite book was about adventurers and explorers and that's the one I always asked to have read to me. **1** I wanted to go to wild places, I knew I would do things no one else had done, like abseil down the highest mountain, or walk to the North Pole with only a polar bear for company.

I used to lie in bed and imagine that I was sleeping in a cabin in the middle of the Amazon Jungle with bears prowling outside, or in a tent in the Sahara Desert with tigers nearby. **2** There aren't any bears in the Amazon, or tigers in the Sahara.

I also used to think about the first sea explorers, sailing from their homes to the ends of the earth, where they thought they might fall off the edge of the world, or be swallowed up by a sea monster. **3** They needed courage and trust to go out into the world. I knew that I wanted to be like that – I'd never be able to just sit around and accept the world as it is.

So I'm always pushing the limits. I always climb the tallest tree rather than the easiest, jump off the cliff into the sea rather than walk down, hold my breath underwater for longer than anyone else, try to cycle down the steepest hill near our house as fast as I can. **4** So I didn't try that again.

A Of course, at some point I realised that I'd got some of those details confused.
B They knew they could be killed at any moment through their lack of knowledge or poor judgement.
C I was aware that they were not the only ones who had done that.
D That last attempt ended in disaster, for the only thing I achieved was broken bones.
E Most of it went over my head, but the main theme stayed with me.

6 Work in pairs. Which words helped you choose? Which sentence doesn't fit and why?

Grammar – Past tenses **G** *See page 79*

7 Read this text about Parker Liautaud and put the verb in brackets into the correct tense (past simple or past perfect).

Parker Liautaud **(1)** ……………… (attempt) to reach the North Pole. Two other teenagers **(2)** ……………… (reach) the North Pole previously. They **(3)** ……………… (travel) with their parents but Parker **(4)** ……………… (go) with a guide called Doug, who **(5)** ……………… (be) to the North Pole seven times before. Unfortunately, the cracks in the ice **(6)** ……………… (be) too large for them to cross. Doug **(7)** ……………… (not see) problems like that before on his other trips. In the end, they **(8)** ……………… (fly) the last part of the journey in a helicopter.

READING AND USE OF ENGLISH

Part 2

Grammar – Tenses and prepositions G *See page 79*

1 ⊙ Choose the correct word or words in italics in these sentences.

1 Yesterday I went shopping and I *'ve bought / bought* two fantastic T-shirts.
2 The shops were closed and we had to wait *to / until* the next day.
3 There were strange noises outside, so I *looked / was looking* out of the window to see what *happened / was happening*.
4 There's nothing to do here *for / during* the winter.
5 I *'ve been trying / tried* to do this homework since I got home and I still *haven't finished / didn't finish*.
6 Last week, as I *was coming / came* home, I *was seeing / saw* a strange animal.
7 There was a long queue because everybody had arrived *at / during* the same time.
8 Suddenly, my father realised he *'d forgotten / forgot* to lock the car.
9 I practised the piano every day *during / for* three weeks.
10 I looked everywhere for my purse but it *had disappeared / disappeared*.

2 Read the text below quickly to find out what it is about. Think about what kind of word is needed for each gap. Most of the missing words are prepositions or parts of verbs.

Exam task

For questions 1–8, think of the word which best fits each gap. Use only one word in each gap. There is an example at the beginning (0). Use the grammar exercise above to help you.

Exam tip ⟩

You only ever need to write one word in the gap. It will never be a contraction like *didn't* as this is really two words (*did not*).

THE MYSTERY OF THE BERMUDA TRIANGLE

The Bermuda Triangle is an imaginary triangle in the Atlantic Ocean. **(0)** ...FOR... many years, people have told stories about mysterious disappearances that have **(1)** .... place in this area.

The explorer Christopher Columbus first wrote about the Bermuda Triangle in 1492. He **(2)** .... sailing across the Atlantic Ocean when he came **(3)** .... some mysterious light patterns in the sky. **(4)** .... the same time, his equipment started doing bizarre things.

It wasn't **(5)** .... the 1950s that the media became interested and journalists published articles highlighting the disappearance of several ships and planes. They **(6)** .... all flown or sailed in the area and **(7)** .... of them was ever seen again. How did this happen? You can blame it on bad weather patterns, hurricanes or strange magnetic forces. Some people **(8)** .... even suggested aliens. Whatever the case, it's one of the great mysteries of our time.

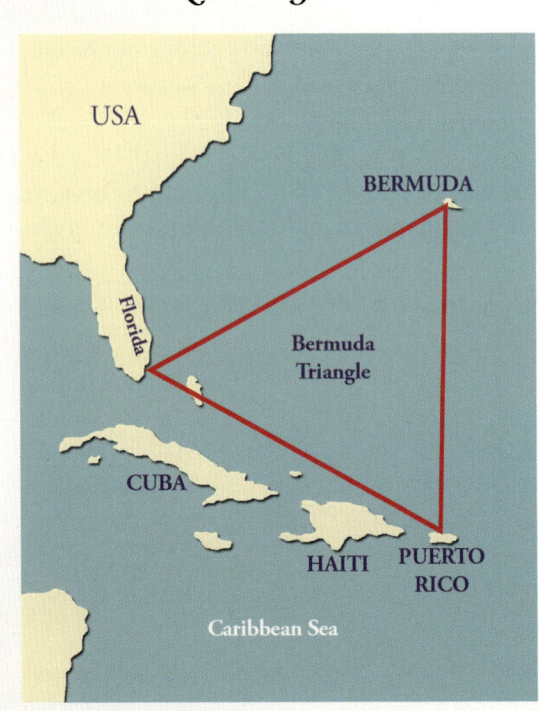

Part 3

Vocabulary – Word building (1)

3 Using the endings in the table, make adjectives from these nouns and verbs. Write them under the best heading.

| accident   adventure   bear   centre   consider   controversy   culture   desire   fashion   forget |
| fury   logic   mystery   nature   predict   rely   remark   suit   universe |

-able	-al	-ous

4 When you check your answers, look carefully at how the spelling changes if the word ends in -y or -e. Write down some examples.

-y: ....

-e: ....

Exam task

For 1–8, read the text below. Use the word given in capitals at the end of some of the lines to form a word that fits in the gap in the same line. There is an example at the beginning (0).

> **Exam tip**
>
> Each gap has its own word at the end of the line that you must change. Don't try to put that word in any other gap.

A TRIP TO REMEMBER

I've just been on a really **(0)** _remarkable_ holiday with my family. My Dad decided that as my sister and I are teenagers now, we could go on a very **(1)** .... holiday. So he found a travel brochure which contained a huge range of **(2)** .... trips, including treks, wildlife encounters and **(3)** .... holidays. We were spoilt for **(4)** .... because there were holidays in all sorts of amazing **(5)** .... , like Peru, India and China. However, in the end we decided to go to South Africa because my sister's a keen **(6)** .... and she was doing a project on the **(7)** .... world, so she wanted to see all the animals. So we saw the sights in Cape Town and then went off to explore Blyde River Canyon, which is one of the largest canyons in the world. It was an absolutely **(8)** .... place; we saw so many animals there.

REMARK

ADVENTURE

EXCITE
CULTURE
CHOOSE

LOCATE

PHOTOGRAPH
NATURE

FORGET

2 SPEAKING

Where you live

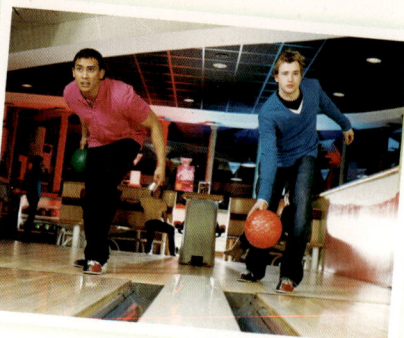

Part 3

1 Think about a city or town you know or have visited. Tick (✔) the places you go/went to.

cinema ☐   café ☐   museum ☐   shopping mall ☐
swimming pool ☐   theatre ☐

Write them in order of importance for you (most important = 1). Add any other leisure facilities you use regularly. Which do you think are most popular with teenagers? Why?

2 Compare your lists in a group. Use some of these expressions.

I think … is the most/least important because …
For me, … is less important than … because …
I'd prefer to go to / I'd rather go to … than … because …
I would like to … but we don't have one.

3 Are there enough things for teenagers to do in your area? Which things would you like to be able to do?

4 You're going to work in a group of three. Think about how you will agree and disagree with the others. Mark these expressions A (agree) or D (disagree).

I don't think that's a good idea. …..   I agree with you. …..
I think it would be better to … …..   That's what I think too. …..
I think you're right. …..   I disagree. …..

Exam task

Work in groups of three. The local council in your town wants to build new leisure facilities for young people. Here are some of the places that the council might build. Talk to each other about whether the places would be popular with teenagers.

- sports centre
- bowling alley
- ice rink
- arts centre
- fast food restaurant

Why might these places be popular with teenagers?

Now decide which two places should be built.

Part 4

5 Do you live in a city, town or village? Tick (✔) the words and expressions below you can use to talk about it.

mining ☐   isolated ☐   quiet ☐
mountain ☐   rural ☐   farming ☐
medium-sized ☐   university ☐
crowded ☐   sleepy ☐   capital ☐
historic ☐   modern ☐   industrial ☐
wide streets ☐   a lot of traffic ☐
in the mountains ☐   not far from … ☐
in the middle of nowhere ☐
by a lake ☐   in the countryside ☐
in the centre of … ☐   on the coast ☐
in an area called … ☐

6 Use the words and expressions from Exercise 5 to answer these questions.

1 How would you describe your city/town/village?

> I live in an industrial city.

> My village is quite isolated.

2 What do you like about the place where you live? What do you dislike about it?

> I love living on the coast.

Exam task

Practise asking your partner his/her opinion on these questions.

- What's the best thing about living in the middle of a city? Why?
- Do you think it's better to live in a city, or in a village in the countryside? Why?
- Is it better for children to grow up in one place or move around? Why?

Exam tip ▸

It is OK to disagree with each other. The discussion is more important than whether you agree.

18 UNIT 2 SPEAKING

2 LISTENING

Part 1

1 Work in pairs. Look at the photos. How are the three cities different?

2 🔘 06 Listen to a teenager talking about the city where she lives. Which city above is she talking about?

Now listen to the recording again. Write down all the words which helped you get the answer and compare with your partner.

3 🔘 07 Read the following example of a Part 1 question. Listen to the recording and answer it.

You hear a girl talking about the city she lives in.
What does she particularly like about it?
A the shopping opportunities
B the different restaurants
C the outdoor festivals

4 🔘 07 Listen again and read the script your teacher gives you. Underline the words which give you the answer. Why are the other answers wrong?

Exam task

In Listening Part 1 you will hear eight recordings and you will answer one question about each. There are four recordings in the task below.

🔘 08 You will hear people talking in four different situations. For questions 1–4, choose the best answer (A, B or C).

1 You hear a boy talking to his aunt about his new school.
What is his opinion of the school?
A The behaviour of students is normally good.
B The design of the building encourages students to study.
C The teachers are better than those at his previous school.

2 You hear two teenagers talking about a film they have just seen.
Which aspect of the film did they both like?
A the humour
B the setting
C the action

3 You hear a girl talking about a school trip she has been on.
What did she learn about on the trip?
A the design of certain textiles
B the life of a designer
C the history of factory design

4 You hear two teenagers talking about a friend.
What do they admire about him?
A He scores lots of goals.
B He encourages other players.
C He is cheerful despite an injury.

LISTENING UNIT 2 19

WRITING

Part 2: Story

1 Work in pairs. Put the pictures in the correct order to tell a story. Begin with picture E.

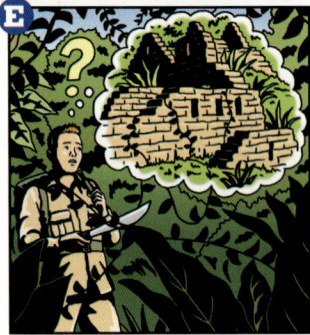

2 Now look at this exam question:

> Your English teacher has asked you to write a story for a competition.
>
> Your story must begin with these words:
> *It was dark and I could hear strange sounds all around me.*
> Your story must include:
> • a jungle
> • treasure
>
> Write your **story**.

In pairs, use the pictures above to explain what happened in the story. Here are some words and phrases to help you. You don't need to write anything.

| archaeologist   expedition   fall into a hole |
| gold   Inca city |

Grammar – Past tenses   *See page 79*

3 Stories are usually written in the past tense. Choose the correct form of the past tense verbs in the story.

> It was dark and I could hear strange sounds all around me. I was in the jungle, **(1)** *looking / looked* for a lost city. Everyone **(2)** *knew / was knowing* it was there, but no one **(3)** *had / has* ever found it. The local people told stories of a city full of gold which the Incas **(4)** *built / had built* centuries ago. Suddenly I **(5)** *heard / was hearing* a different sound and I **(6)** *was realising / realised* that it must be Kate. Kate **(7)** *was / had been* another archaeologist who was part of our expedition. 'Kate, is that you?' I **(8)** *was calling / called*. 'Yeah, come over here, I **(9)** *'ve / 'd* found a plate or something,' she replied. I **(10)** *was rushing / rushed* over to find Kate, without looking where I **(11)** *went / was going* and without warning I **(12)** *'ve disappeared / disappeared* down into a deep hole. Fortunately, I **(13)** *didn't / hadn't* hurt myself. I **(14)** *got out / had got out* my torch and **(15)** *shone / was shining* it around the hole. Gold! Piles and piles of gold plates, vases, jewellery, swords! I **(16)** *'ve / 'd* found it – the treasure everyone **(17)** *had / has* been looking for!

4 Divide the story above into three paragraphs, one for each section of the story.

5 Here are two more exam story questions. How will the stories continue? How could they end? Discuss your ideas with your partner.

A
Your story must begin with these words:
Max heard someone calling his name excitedly, and turned to see who it was.
Your story must include:
• a friend
• a prize

B
Your story must begin with these words:
I was amazed when I saw who was sitting in the seat opposite mine.
Your story must include:
• a journey
• a famous person

Vocabulary – Adverbs and adjectives

6 Match the correct adjective with the noun in these sentences.

> courageous   intriguing   strong   worrying

1 Andrew suddenly had a(n) .... thought – what if the test was today?
2 Paula made a(n) .... attempt to win the marathon, but was beaten by her rival.
3 It's a(n) .... question, and I really want to know the answer to it.
4 When I walked into the room, I had a(n) .... sense that something was wrong.

> aggressive   brilliant   detailed   successful

5 Joanna made a(n) .... attempt on the school javelin record.
6 Max's .... attitude got him into a lot of trouble during his school years.
7 It was a(n) .... solution to the problem, so we decided to put it into effect immediately.
8 The deputy head drew up a(n) .... plan outlining every aspect of English teaching for the year.

7 Choose the correct adverb to go with the verb in these sentences.

1 The headmaster spoke *bitterly / calmly* to the little boy and he soon settled down.
2 The audience reacted very *positively / optimistically* to the second contestant in the talent competition.
3 Our teacher acted *carelessly / decisively* when she heard the fire bell and got everybody out of the school building immediately.
4 Patrick moved forward *clumsily / rapidly* and scored the goal that won the match.
5 All the parents were pleased that the prize-giving ceremony was run very *efficiently / poorly*.
6 Lucy sat in the dentist's surgery waiting *patiently / reliably* for her appointment.
7 The science teacher told his pupils to watch *hopefully / closely* as he carried out the experiment.
8 My best friend made an effort to visit me *rarely / regularly* when I was in hospital for a while.

> **Exam tip**
>
> Your story will read better and get a better mark if you can use some interesting and varied vocabulary and use words that go together well. These are known as collocations.

Grammar – Adverb formation

G *See page 79*

8 Make adjectives from these adverbs.

1 bitterly ....
2 clumsily ....
3 happily ....
4 hopefully ....
5 miserably ....
6 positively ....
7 politely ....
8 rapidly ....
9 rarely ....
10 simply ....

Now use the adverbs and adjectives above to answer these questions.

1 Which adjectives change their last letter to *-i* before adding *-ly*?
2 What happens to adjectives ending in a consonant and *-le*?
3 What happens to other adjectives ending in *-e*?
4 What happens to adjectives ending in *-l*?

Exam task

Write one of the stories, A or B, in Exercise 5 for homework. Remember to:

- decide on your storyline before you start writing.
- make sure your story follows from the prompt sentence.
- use the past tenses and write in paragraphs.
- try to use a range of interesting adjectives, adverbs and collocations.
- write 140–190 words.

W *See pages 87–88*

3 The entertainment industry
LISTENING

A   B   C   D

Films

Part 4

1 Work in pairs. Complete the table with the words and phrases connected with making a film.

acts   arranges the scenery   checks quality of voice recording
designs/fits costumes   does action shots
does someone's face/hair   films a scene   performs
plays a part/role   raises money to make the film
takes a shot of something   tells the actors what to do

Person	What (s)he does
actor	acts,
stuntman/woman	
set decorator	
director	
cameraman/woman	
producer	
costume designer	
sound technician	
make-up artist	

2 The people in the pictures work in the film industry. Use the words above to describe them and say what they are doing.

3 Look at the Exam task opposite and the underlining in question 1. Underline two or three important words in the instructions and in the other questions and options.

4 What do the instructions and questions tell you about what you will hear? Tick (✓) the topics you think Tania will talk about.

how she became famous ☐
a problem she has had ☐
her reactions to her own acting ☐
her opinion of the director ☐
her own personality ☐
her daily routine ☐
her favourite film ☐

Exam task

In Listening Part 4 there are seven multiple-choice questions. In the task below there are four.

🔊 09 You will hear part of an interview with a young actor called Tania West. For questions 1–4, choose the best answer (A, B or C).

1 Tania describes seeing herself on screen as
   A rather frightening.
   B slightly unreal.
   C a bit boring.

2 In what way is Tania like Angie, the character she plays in the film?
   A She doesn't get on well with other people.
   B She doesn't try to impress people.
   C She doesn't always behave as other people expect.

3 What did Tania find difficult about being on set?
   A working with older actors
   B learning her lines
   C having little time to relax

4 What does Tania say about her acting schedule?
   A She often filmed at night.
   B She had little trouble getting up early.
   C She missed having regular meals.

Exam tip ›

Underlining important words helps you to listen for the answer and predict what you will hear.

3 WRITING

Part 2: Review

1 Work in pairs. Answer the questions below.

1 What is your favourite type of film? Tick (✔) the one(s) you like best.

action films ☐ animations ☐ cartoons ☐ comedies ☐ documentaries ☐
horror films ☐ romantic comedies (romcoms) ☐ science fiction films ☐
thrillers ☐ westerns ☐

2 What makes a film enjoyable? Tick (✔) the things you think are most important.

the acting ☐ the casting ☐ the direction ☐ the location ☐ the music ☐
the plot ☐ the script ☐ the special effects ☐ the stunts ☐

2 Look at the photos and discuss the questions in pairs.

1 Do you recognise the heroes? Who are they? Who is your favourite hero?
2 Do you have any special heroes, real or imaginary, in your country? Describe them.

3 Read the Exam task below and answer the questions.

1 Can you write about a comedy, thriller or horror film? Yes or no? Why?
2 Can you write a negative opinion of the film? Yes or no? Why?

> Your English teacher has asked you to write a review for the film club website of a film which has an impressive hero. Describe the film and the hero. Say what happens in the film and explain whether you would recommend it to other people.

4 Read the exam candidate's review and answer the questions.

1 Does the review give a clear impression of the film and the characters in it?
2 Does it make you want to see the film? Why? / Why not?
3 What tense is used in the review? Could you use any other tense?
4 Why does the review have a title?
5 Which sentence sums up the candidate's opinion?

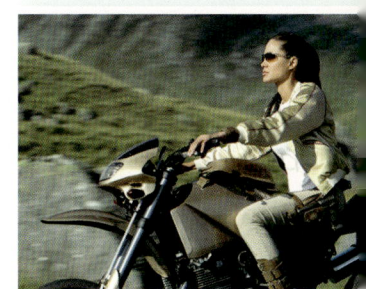

BATMAN: THE DARK KNIGHT

This is a classic in the Batman series. It is a dark, difficult and at times rather disturbing film, which really makes you think. As you sit in the audience, you wonder what would happen if a hero like Batman really came along and decided to deal with organised crime in our big cities, yet you are also entertained because the film has a lot of amazing action scenes.

In The Dark Knight, Batman is an action hero, but more importantly he is also a symbol of justice. He is a brave and determined character who teams up with the forces of law and order in the city of Gotham, ready to take on all the crime lords. As a result, he has to face a psychopathic and very scary villain called The Joker.

In my opinion, this film is outstanding. It is not only thrilling but it also makes you feel as if you are experiencing what is going on. When I saw it, everyone in the audience was totally involved in it, so I'd say it's a film you really must see.

5 Underline the adjectives and phrases the candidate uses to describe the film, Batman and the Joker. Write them under the correct heading. Is each one positive (P) or negative (N)?

Film   Batman   Joker

dark (N)

6 You should always write a brief plan before you start writing. Complete this plan for the review of Batman: The Dark Knight.

BATMAN: THE DARK KNIGHT

Para 1 introduction – describe the film, makes you .... + amazing .... scenes
Para 2 content of film – describe Batman and his .... and how he fights organised .... and The ....
Para 3 conclusion – sum up film and .... it (explain why)

7 Underline any linking words/phrases in the review which you could use yourself.

It is not only thrilling, but it also makes you …

8 Look back at the types of film you ticked in Exercise 1 (page 23). Which film would you write about if you had to write a review of one of them? Tell your partner.

Exam task

Choose one of the exam tasks below. Decide which film you are going to write about and write your plan (three paragraphs) before writing your review, in 140–190 words.

1 You have seen this English-language advertisement in a magazine called *Film*.

Film reviews wanted! The best thriller ever

Have you seen a really exciting thriller recently? Write a review telling us about it. You should include information about the plot, the action scenes and the characters, and tell us whether you would recommend the film.

The best film reviews will be posted on our website next month.

Write your review.

2 You have seen this announcement in an international magazine for teenagers.

Film reviews wanted! Romantic comedies

Have you seen a really enjoyable romantic comedy recently? Write a review telling us about the characters and what happens in the film, and say whether you would recommend the film to your friends.

The best reviews will be published in our magazine next month.

Write your review.

- Make sure you give the name of the film.
- Plan your writing; write at least three paragraphs.
- Try to use some colourful vocabulary from the unit.
- Use some of the linking words/phrases from the unit.
- Write 140–190 words (at least 170 words if you can).

W See page 88

3 READING AND USE OF ENGLISH

Music

Part 7

1 Answer the questions below and then compare your answers with a partner.

1 What sort of music do you like best? Why?

> pop   heavy metal   rock 'n' roll   classical   jazz   rap
> hip hop   salsa   punk   soul music

2 Look at the picture. Which instruments would a rock band, a jazz band and a classical orchestra use?

2 Read the statements and the album review below. Tick (✔) the statements which match information in the review. Put a cross against the statements which say something different.

The album

contains songs whose words will appeal to a certain age group.	1
contains songs which will tend to have a negative effect on people's emotions.	2
will probably be less well received than the band's last one.	3
takes a completely different approach from the band's last one.	4
is likely to extend the success of the band.	5
has a singer whose particular style has been well matched to the songs he sings.	6
has a singer who should be given more chances to sing.	7

Probable and Possible by Miracle

All the songs on this album have lyrics which focus on the kinds of emotions that teenagers will really relate to but there's no way you could describe it as depressing.
Last autumn, the band Miracle brought out a long-awaited album which upset a lot of fans because it introduced a whole new sound. However, that album brought in new fans like me. *Probable and Possible* develops that sound and is expected to further widen the band's appeal, so it seems things can only get better for them from here. Bradley, one of the singers, has a very unusual voice and he needs the right song. He only sings on a couple of tracks but they suit him perfectly. The rest of the singing is done by Kez, whose voice is amazing. Overall, there is almost nothing to criticise.

3 Quickly read through the texts on page 26 and answer these questions.
Spend only three minutes reading the texts.

1 Are the reviews all positive?
2 Would you like to listen to any of these albums?
3 Do any of them sound like albums you already listen to?

Exam task

In Reading and Use of English Part 7 there are between four and six texts and you answer ten questions. The texts below are shorter and there are only eight questions.

You are going to read some reviews of music albums. For questions 1–8, choose from the albums (A–D). The albums may be chosen more than once.

Which album

might be difficult to follow with one of the same quality?	1
contains songs which can sound quite similar to each other?	2
contains songs about subjects often avoided?	3
features a performer who will continue to appeal to the same people in future years?	4
would be improved without the inclusion of certain songs?	5
has been looked forward to for some time?	6
has a song which stands out, but not because everyone will recognise it?	7
has songs which are unusual in combining both excellent music and words?	8

Grammar – Linking words G *See page 80*

4 👁 The underlined linking words in these sentences are used incorrectly. Find examples in the texts where they are used correctly. Then correct the mistakes.

1 <u>While</u> the fact that we were given a lot of homework, I managed to finish it all.
2 I like cycling to school. <u>Although</u> I don't like cycling in heavy traffic.
3 I took my brother to see a western <u>despite</u> I don't like westerns myself.
4 <u>However</u> I enjoyed the concert, I wouldn't say it was the best I'd been to.
5 In the winter I play football. <u>In spite of</u> in the summer I play tennis too.
6 <u>Even though</u> playing the guitar very well, Anita has never learnt to read music.

THIS WEEK'S BEST ALBUM RELEASES

A ***Pedal Street* by Breeze**
Reviewer Anna Martino, age 13

Breeze has released *Pedal Street* after a two-year wait, in spite of pressure from fans and their record company to do so earlier. Fans had been told to expect something special and this is a masterpiece. With drummer Tom Wiseman's strong rhythms, and bassist Miguel Sandro's fantastic harmonies, this band's music is exceptional. The song lyrics express emotions that are felt by everybody, focusing on topics other artists seem to prefer not to sing about. Lead singer Josh Smith's voice is so emotional that it feels as though he's sitting right in front of you. Breeze use an interesting mix of styles including classical strings and modern guitar riffs.

B ***Thrill* by Skydiggers**
Reviewer Alexis Walker, age 14

Skydiggers, a Canadian rock group, have released the album *Thrill*, which was recorded over two years. Suzi Tarrant begins with high-pitched, smooth vocals, drawing you into the soft sound of her voice. However, she then shows just what the band is about with the roaring, angry growl that follows. Although some tunes are difficult to distinguish from each other in the sense that Tarrant's voice doesn't vary from song to song, the album will soon be permanently fixed on your playlist. On many albums, the best song is not the most well known and that is certainly the case here – the song 'Up to here' is in a class of its own.

C ***Silver Honeybees* by Lena and the Lantanas**
Reviewer Sam Roberts, age 16

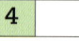

Lena and her band, the Lantanas, tie together both contemporary and soul music in this album. Lena has been allowed to sing all types of songs here, including acoustic ballads and jazz-pop, in order to really show what she can do. And in case you think that her new far-ranging style may not be attractive to a youthful teenage fan base, remember that her teen audience is sure to mature and grow along with her as she makes more music. While some bands incorporate good beats but have cliché lyrics that make you feel slightly sick, or sing songs with meaningful words yet make a dreadful sound, the Lantanas are by contrast a rare find.

D ***Hungry Rock* by April Sapa**
Reviewer Julie Zhang, age 14

April Sapa's début album shows her liking for punk, which she mixes with pop-rock. This first album will set high standards for her second, but it also shows that she has room to grow. Despite having a more limited vocal range than her sister, who is also a singer, April proves that she does have a big talent for writing. The album covers everything a teenager can feel: love, hate, acceptance, defiance and even boredom. It is an excellent combination of easy listening, even though there are several songs that could easily have been left out, resulting in a better album overall.

3 SPEAKING

What might people enjoy about these different types of film?

Why is music important to these different groups of people?

Part 1

1 Look at question 1 and the candidate's answer below. Then write your answers for questions 1–6, add extra information and an additional comment and/or opinion.

Films and Cinema
1 Do you usually watch films on television, or at the cinema?
2 If you go to the cinema, when do you go, and who with?
3 What is your favourite type of film and why?

Music
4 Have you ever been to a concert? Did you enjoy it?
5 When and how do you like listening to music?
6 Do you play a musical instrument? Which one?

[extra information] [answer]

I don't live near a cinema so I watch a lot of films on TV and DVD. It's a great way to relax in the evening and I like to watch with my family or friends.

[additional comment/opinion]

2 Now take it in turns to ask each other the questions.

> **Exam tip**
>
> Don't just give one-word answers. Try to give extra information. Then add a comment or opinion.

Part 2

3 Work in pairs. Make a list of things you can say about the pictures above.

4 🔊 10 Now listen to two candidates talking about the pictures. Did they have the same ideas as you? Tick (✔) the ideas that are on your list.

5 🔊 10 Listen again. Both the candidates needed words they didn't know. Complete the phrases they used to explain what they meant.

1 … you know, the .... films which have .... , not actors
2 … these people are … well, ... a bank has just been robbed or .... that.
3 It's a .... street dance I don't know the .... of …
4 … the children in the photo of the school orchestra, they look very … well … er … um .... relaxed.

6 The candidates avoided four words they didn't know. What were they?

7 🔊 11 Listen to the last part of each conversation again and tick (✔) the phrases the candidates used to answer these questions.

Which of these films would you prefer to see?
Which of the activities would you prefer to do?
I'd rather … than … ☐   I'd prefer to … ☐   I'd sooner … ☐
I think it's better to … ☐   I'd definitely … ☐

Exam task

Now you are each going to talk about two of the pictures for one minute. Ask your partner the question above the pictures and time him/her for one minute.

> **Exam tip**
>
> If you don't know a word, use a phrase to explain it.

SPEAKING UNIT 3   27

READING AND USE OF ENGLISH

Part 4

Grammar – The passive *See page 80*

1 **10** Look at these sentences from Speaking Part 2. Complete them with the correct tense of the passive. Check your answers by listening again.

Candidate A
1 … a mouse .... by a cat and I suppose .... soon.
2 … a bank .... or something like that. That's why the men in the black car .... by the police. They .... (probably) soon and .... to the police station.

Candidate B
3 The music .... on a sound system with huge speakers.
4 I guess some of them .... to do it by their parents or teacher.
5 … I expect the concert .... by the parents.

2 Now write the verbs from Exercise 1 in the correct column in the table. (You won't find an example of every tense.)

	verb form	past participle
present simple		
present continuous	is/are being	chased
future simple		
past simple		
present perfect		
past perfect		
with modals		

3 There are eight more examples of the passive in Reading and Use of English Part 7 on page 26 (look at both the questions and the texts). Underline them and add them to the table.

4 **Ⓞ** Now correct the mistakes with the passive in these sentences written by exam candidates.

1 This castle has been builded in the twelfth century.
2 I was give a leaflet which contained some interesting information.
3 The band first established in 1992.
4 These days music has been making by computers.
5 My best friend called Ann-Marie.
6 The concert supposed to start at 7.00, but the guitarist arrived late.
7 My house located in a beautiful area.
8 The business studies course cancelled at the last minute.
9 Will lunch include in the price of the school trip?
10 My family stay in a house that situated a few miles from the beach.

5 In Reading and Use of English Part 4 you have to complete a sentence using a prompt word, so that it means the same as the original above it. You can write only two to five words in the gap. Choose the correct answer for these examples. Why are the other answers wrong?

1 A number of reviewers on teenage websites have strongly recommended Tom Cox's new book.
   BEEN
   Tom Cox's new book .... on teenage websites.
   A has been strongly recommended
   B had been strongly recommended
   C is being strongly recommended

2 Everyone was disappointed when the head teacher cancelled the trip at the last moment.
   WAS
   To everyone's .... by the head teacher at the last moment.
   A disappointed the trip was cancelled
   B disappointment the trip was cancelled
   C disappointment the trip had to be cancelled

3 We thought the school concert was going to end at 9.00, but it didn't finish until 10.00.
   SUPPOSED
   The school concert .... finished at 9.00 but it went on until 10.00.
   A is supposed to be
   B was supposed to
   C was supposed to be

4 My older brother has got a job interview tomorrow.
   BEING
   My older brother .... a job tomorrow.
   A is being interviewed for
   B being interviewed for
   C is being interviewed to

5 I'd prefer to watch the football on TV tonight.
   RATHER
   I .... the football on TV tonight.
   A 'd rather to watch
   B rather to watch
   C 'd rather watch

Exam task

Complete the second sentence so that it has a similar meaning to the first sentence, using the word given. Do not change the word given. You must use between two and five words, including the word given.

Exam tip

If you have written more than five words (a word like *I've* counts as two words), you have made a mistake.

1 The Romans constructed this wall nearly 2000 years ago.
   BUILT
   This wall .... the Romans nearly 2000 years ago.

2 A small boy on a skateboard knocked my sister over yesterday.
   WAS
   My sister .... a small boy on a skateboard yesterday.

3 The radio stations have played that music track over a hundred times this week.
   HAS
   That music track .... than a hundred times this week by the radio stations.

4 By this time next week we'll have given all our projects to our English teacher.
   HANDED
   By this time next week all our projects .... to our English teacher.

5 Anna Hamilton will wear one of Dior's dresses to the opening night.
   BE
   One of Dior's dresses .... Anna Hamilton to the opening night.

6 Our teacher won't give us so much homework next weekend as it's a national holiday.
   LESS
   We .... homework by our teacher next weekend as it's a national holiday.

4 Active life
READING AND USE OF ENGLISH

Part 5

1 Look at the list of sports below. Which do you think are the five most popular sports in the world? Which sports are most popular in your country?

.... athletics	.... badminton	.... cricket
.... cycling	.... football	.... gymnastics
.... hockey	.... ice skating	.... martial arts
.... snowboarding	.... surfing	.... tennis
.... volleyball	.... windsurfing	.... yoga

2 We do athletics, we play badminton and we go cycling. Write the correct verb in Exercise 1. Add any other sports that you enjoy to the list.

3 Look at the sports in Exercise 1 and answer the questions.

1 Have you ever done any of them?
2 Do you enjoy watching any of them?
3 Which sport(s) would you like to try?
4 Who is your favourite sportsperson and why?

4 Which words in the box below can you use to talk about football / tennis? Three words don't match either sport. What kind of sport are they used for?

court   defender   goalkeeper   lap   net
opponent   penalty   pitch   point   race
referee   serve   tackle   track   umpire

5 Read the text *Future football stars* quickly to get an idea of what it is about.

Which paragraph …

A makes a comparison between success in football and in other areas?
B describes the advantages of being at a football academy?
C suggests how some boys react when they are chosen for a football academy?
D explains what a football academy is?

30 UNIT 4 READING AND USE OF ENGLISH

Exam task

In Reading and Use of English Part 5 there is a long text and there are six questions based on it. The text below is shorter and there are four questions on it.

> **Exam tip**
>
> There are usually one or two questions about each paragraph. The questions are always in the same order as the text.

You are going to read an extract from a newspaper article. For questions 1–4, choose the answer (A, B, C or D) which you think fits best according to the text.

FUTURE FOOTBALL STARS

Football academies were set up by leading football clubs like Manchester United and Liverpool so their coaches could run trials to identify and train talented boys from as young as eight as potential players for their first team. All the big football clubs have one, and other less well-known teams run their own schools of excellence.

_{line 5}

This means that in Britain there are at least 9,000 boys at any one time attending academies after school who think they are going to be a famous footballer. Unfortunately, for most this isn't the case. One eight-year-old was selected for Chelsea academy and he went from being top of his class at school to being the boy who was messing around at the back. His mother asked him why he wasn't trying hard at school any more. His reply was that he was going to be a goalkeeper and be rich, so he didn't need to. In the end, he only lasted a year in the academy but, luckily for him, he was still young enough to recover and not be so discouraged that he never played football again.

But football is not unique. Any sport or other activity where only a few can get to the top has an invisible layer of also-rans. These people are very talented and do their absolute best but ultimately it will not pay off because they are just not exceptional enough. In football, this effect is magnified because the number of players selected for training by academies is so huge. Most of these won't get into a team and most won't become professionals.

This doesn't put off all the boys who are spotted by the big football clubs and are desperate to join the academies. The benefits are still there for them of course. They get to play as much football as possible – the coaches teach them to pass, tackle and practise standard techniques, moves and penalty kicks over and over again. The skills become part of them, as they are with professional players, so they are automatic and the boys don't have to think about them when they're on the pitch. Experts say this is the way to do it, otherwise you end up with players who are much more likely to get injured.

Before you decide on your answer to each question, read the tip above it to help you.

> Underline 'one', then read the text before and after that word. The words in the options are all in the text.

1 What does 'one' refer to in line 5?
 A a trial
 B a coach
 C a first team
 D an academy

> Find the reference to the boy's mother. Read the whole paragraph before answering the question.

2 What did one boy's mother notice after he joined an academy?
 A His schoolwork suffered because football took up too much time.
 B There was little support at school for his changed circumstances.
 C There was a significant change in his attitude towards school.
 D He refused to play football at school any more.

> Find 'an invisible layer of also-rans' and underline it. Don't worry if you don't understand it as it will be explained in the text. Underline the explanation and then answer the question.

3 What is the writer referring to by 'an invisible layer of also-rans' in the third paragraph?
 A those footballers who will not in the end be rewarded for their hard work
 B the fact that there are fewer opportunities for professional footballers than there used to be
 C the number of footballers who are not willing to put in the amount of effort required
 D the fact that the wrong people are sometimes selected to play in the best teams

> There are several benefits mentioned in the text. Which one matches one of the options?

4 What advantage of the academies is mentioned in the fourth paragraph?
 A The coaches can adapt techniques to suit individual players.
 B The players are trained in a way which results in fewer injuries.
 C There are experts to answer the players' questions.
 D There are more opportunities to watch professional players in action.

4 LISTENING

Part 2

1 Read these sentences about a girl who rides mountain bikes. Which one needs an adjective in the gap?

FREYA STANLEY – DOWNHILL MOUNTAIN BIKER

Freya was given her first mountain bike by her **(1)** ....

Freya nearly lost her last race because of a **(2)** ....

The last thing Freya checks before a race is the **(3)** ....

Freya thinks the most important thing about clothes is that they are **(4)** ....

2 Which gap in Exercise 1 could each of these words go in?

brakes   brother   comfortable   friend   photographer
post   rock   route   sister   stylish   tight   tree   tyres
uncle   warm   weather

3 🔊 **12** Listen to Freya. Choose the word she says for each gap.

Exam task

In Listening Part 2 you will hear a long recording and answer ten questions on it. The task below has six questions.

🔊 **13** You will hear part of a talk by a young skater called Karl Milton. For questions 1–6, complete the sentences with a word or short phrase.

KARL MILTON – SKATER

Karl came in **(1)** .... place in a competition last week.

The most important thing for skaters when practising is to remember to **(2)** ....

Karl thinks about the **(3)** ....when he is performing in a competition.

Karl will appear in a TV programme called **(4)** ....

In the TV show competitors can choose their own **(5)** ....

Going **(6)** ....in his spare time benefits Karl's skating skills.

> **Exam tip**
>
> You usually need to write one word but sometimes you will write two or three words. The word(s) you write should be exactly what you hear.

Grammar – Modal verbs

 See page 81

4 Complete Karl's sentences with one of the modal verbs given. Listen again if you need to.

can   can't   have to   should

1 You .... build up your confidence.
2 They .... choose who they skate with.
3 They .... follow a certain routine.
4 They .... decide which music they want to skate to.

could have won   should have been
must have been practising

5 I .... in the team four years ago.
6 Jack Graham .... all the time as he was even better than last year.
7 Either of us .... but you just never know who's going to do best on the day.

5 Which sentence in Exercise 4 mentions something which:

is allowed ....   seems certain ....
is advised ....   isn't allowed ....
was possible ....   is a rule ....
was expected ....

6 👁 Now choose the correct verb in these sentences.

1 My family go for a walk on Sundays when we *mustn't / don't have to* work.
2 The show *must / should* have started at 7.30 but it started at 8.15.
3 I don't remember the date but it *should / must* have been a Friday.
4 You *mustn't / don't have to* miss the chance to see this amazing film.
5 He *must / had to* be quick because he didn't have much time to get there.
6 The first time Steve was late, his mother thought that something *must / should* have happened to him.

32   UNIT 4   LISTENING

4 SPEAKING

Part 3

1 Which of the above activities would you choose to get fit? Which would you choose to have fun? Discuss with a partner. For each one, think about:

- how fit you need to be to do the activity and how easy it is to learn
- if you can do the activity with other people and how competitive it is
- if you would like to do the activity regularly

2 Now change partners and do the Exam task below. Your discussion should last for about three minutes. Time yourselves.

Here are some useful expressions.

Asking your partner's opinion	Reacting to your partner
What do you think?	Do you think so?
What would you choose?	Really?
How about you?	It's not the same for me because …
Do you think it's best to …?	I feel the same because …
Shall we start with …?	

Exam task

Many students do sport at school. Here are some ideas for you to think about and a question for you to discuss.

Now decide how often students should do sport at school each week.

Part 4

3 In Speaking Part 4 you are asked for your opinions on a topic connected with Speaking Part 3, for example:

Do you think people of your age do enough sport or do they prefer to watch TV?

Look at these opinions. Do you agree with any of them?

> It's much easier to watch TV or go on the computer than make an effort to do sport.

> It can be expensive to do sport because you have to pay for somewhere to play.

> Well, teenagers do watch a lot of TV but watching sport on TV encourages you to go and do it.

> I think the problem is that there aren't enough places to do sport.

4 Can you think of other answers to the question?

Exam tip

The examiner will ask you several questions so the discussion lasts for four minutes. Don't worry if you can't think of more to say as there will be another question.

Exam task

Work in pairs to answer the questions.

- Should there be more opportunities to do different sports at school? Why / Why not?
- Why are some sports less popular than others?
- How can people who don't like competitive sport be encouraged to get fit? Why is that a good idea?

READING AND USE OF ENGLISH

Part 2

Keeping fit and healthy

Grammar – Prepositions following verbs and adjectives

1 👁 **Choose the correct preposition in these sentences.**

1 What happens now depends *on / of* what our teacher decides.
2 Parents are responsible *of / for* what their children do.
3 José always had excellent marks so I was very jealous *of / about* him.
4 I would like to help *for / with* the concert tonight.
5 When children get bored they start complaining *about / for* everything.
6 The dance I did is typical *of / from* the south of Spain.
7 I've been thinking *about / of* your problem and what you should do.
8 I'm so excited *for / about* the party tomorrow.
9 I'm very interested *in / about* learning the guitar.
10 I talked *at / to* my friends about your idea and they want to come.

> **Exam tip**
> Learn verbs and adjectives with their prepositions as they are often tested in Reading and Use of English Part 2.

> **Exam tip**
> Read the text quickly first, then write the missing words in the gaps. When you have finished, read the whole text again. Check that the words you've written make sense.

Exam task

For questions 1–8, read the text below and think of the word which best fits each gap. Use only one word in each gap. There is an example at the beginning (0).

ENJOYABLE EXERCISE

You (0) ...have... probably heard countless times how exercise will keep you fit and healthy. But getting (1) .... right amount can also increase your energy levels and even help improve your mood too. Experts recommend that teenagers get 60 minutes (2) .... more of physical activity every day. Many teenagers achieve this by getting involved (3) .... sports at school and team sports especially can be fun. Some people aren't keen (4) .... playing team sports, however, and may not be very good at them. But (5) .... are plenty of other ways you can get aerobic exercise on (6) .... own or with friends by doing activities (7) .... as cycling, running, swimming, dancing and walking. Try to have fun at the same time and then you will feel (8) .... doing exercise instead of thinking it is something you have to do. Everyone can find something that suits them.

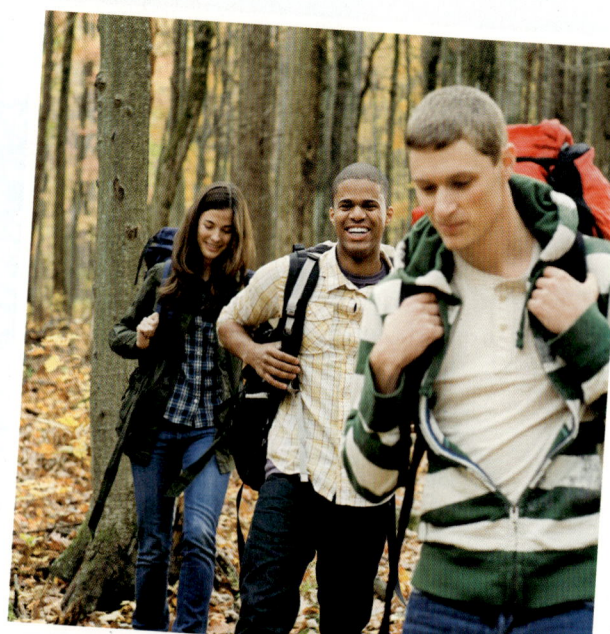

Part 3

Vocabulary – Word building (2)

2 Look at the words in the second column. Make a noun from each one and write the suffix in the last column.

		Noun	Noun suffix
Adjectives	SILENT	silence	t + ce
	SIMILAR		
Verbs	CONCLUDE		
	SUGGEST		

> **Exam tip**
> You may need to add some extra letters or change some letters before you add a suffix.

3 Make nouns from these words, using the suffixes from Exercise 2.

Adjectives: confident convenient curious equal generous independent patient possible
Verbs: appreciate concentrate connect decorate divide expand produce react

Exam task

For questions 1–8, read the text below. Use the word given in capitals at the end of some of the lines to form a word that fits in the gap in the same line. There is an example at the beginning (0).

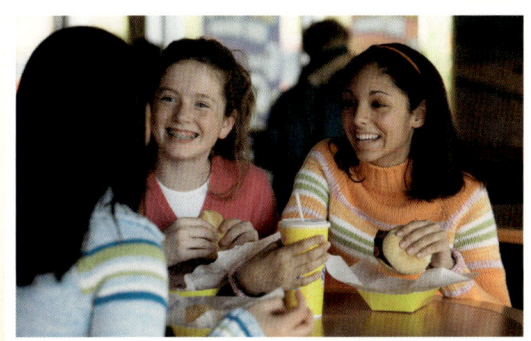

THE FAST FOOD REVOLUTION

Fast food was not **(0)** *fashionable* worldwide until the 1970s but, in fact, fast food restaurants existed in the US long before that. Drive-in restaurants opened in the 1940s as restaurant owners took advantage of the growing **(1)** .... of cars. Meals were designed so that knives, spoons or forks were not needed – a concept which sounded like **(2)** .... at the time to people who were used to eating at a table. The restaurants were **(3)** .... however and this led to fast food becoming **(4)** .... common around the world. Today, most cities have a wide **(5)** .... of fast food restaurants, although drive-in restaurants are not popular everywhere. The most recent trend has been the **(6)** .... of options like salads and fish to menus, giving diners a wider **(7)** .... Another change has taken place because there is more interest in protecting the environment. Many restaurants now use recycled packaging as it has become **(8)** .... for so much packaging to just be thrown away.

FASHION

POPULAR

MAD

SUCCESS
INCREASE
VARY

INTRODUCE
CHOOSE
ACCEPT

Vocabulary – Food

4 Make adjectives that you can use to describe food from these nouns.

| fat nut salt spice taste |

5 Which of the adjectives in the box can you use with the nouns below? (You can use some of the adjectives twice.)

.... diet .... meat .... fruit .... pudding

| balanced fried healthy low-fat raw rich |
| ripe rotten seasonal sugary tough vegetarian |

4 WRITING

Part 2: Letter and email

1 Read this exam question.

> You have received a letter from your English-speaking pen friend.
>
> I start at my new school soon, and I discovered yesterday that we all have to do sport on Wednesday afternoons. As you know, I'm not that keen on sport, but at least I've got the choice of doing volleyball, tennis or athletics. Have you done any of these? Which is easiest? Which do you think I should choose?
>
> Write soon,
>
> Alex

With your partner discuss what advice you would give Alex. Use these phrases.

> I'd advise/recommend him to …
> I'd suggest/recommend … -ing
> He could/should …

2 Read this reply. Put these phrases in the gaps.

it'd be better to   don't worry too much about
remember that   it should   I suggest you   why not
you can   recommend doing

> Hi Alex,
> The first thing I'd say is **(1)** ………………………………………………
> having to do a sport. I know you've never been particularly sporty, but there'll be other people like you! Anyway, just
> **(2)** ……………………………………… doing sport is a great way to make friends, so **(3)** ……………………………………… turn out to be a positive experience in the end!
>
> I've played a lot of tennis, and learning all the different strokes takes a very long time. It's really difficult, so perhaps **(4)** ……………………………………… do something else. Athletics can be fun, but a lot of the people who take it up are very serious, and go in for competitions and so on. For that reason, **(5)** ……………………………………… avoid it.
>
> **(6)** ……………………………………… take up volleyball? I'd **(7)** ……………………………………… a team sport because you're bound to meet lots of people, which is a good thing when you're starting at a new school. Best of all, **(8)** ……………………………………… have fun even if you don't play brilliantly. That's because compared to tennis and athletics, it really isn't difficult to learn. I often play volleyball with friends at the weekend, and in the summer we occasionally play on the beach.
>
> Good luck with everything – and let me know how it goes!
> Pete

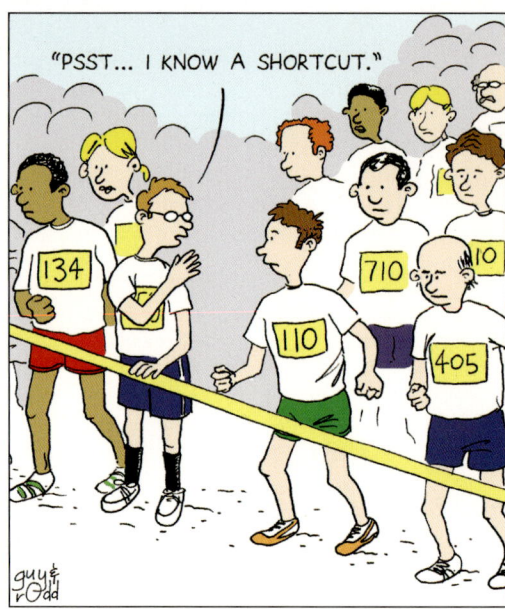

3 Read Pete's letter again. Are these sentences true or false?

1 He begins his letter with some general advice.
2 He talks about two of the three sports Alex mentions.
3 He doesn't give reasons for the advice he gives.
4 He talks about his own experience of sport.
5 He finishes his letter by repeating his advice.
6 He has written in an appropriate style.

> **Exam tip** ›
>
> The layout of letters and emails is different, but the technique is the same: answer the questions and give information or make suggestions as required (without adding any irrelevant information).

4 Now read this exam question.

> You have received an email from your English-speaking friend.
>
> Help! My parents keep telling me that I spend too much time indoors studying, and they've asked me to think of some fun activities to do outdoors. Have you got any suggestions? They could be things to do with family and friends, or things to do on my own.
> Thanks!
> Annie

What activities would you suggest for Annie? Discuss your ideas with a partner.

36   UNIT 4   WRITING

5 Read this reply. Some sentences are missing. Decide which sentence A–E fits best in gaps 1–5.

> Hi Annie
>
> Why don't you go for a bike ride somewhere nice and peaceful outside town? Or you could just go walking if you prefer. **(1)** .... We usually take a picnic with us. In the summer, when it's warmer, we also go to the beach and swim or fly the huge kite that I got for my birthday last year. **(2)** ....
>
> I'd also recommend taking up an outdoor sport if you don't do one. What about tennis? As you know, it's one of my favourite sports. Or you could always give sailing a try. **(3)** .... And how about taking up running? **(4)** .... You can listen to your music as you go! It's a great way to get fit, and you'll feel cheerful and positive at the end of each run.
>
> **(5)** .... Get back to me if you'd like any more.
>
> Love, Susie x

A If you take a course at the weekend at a local club it's not too expensive.
B I hope some of the suggestions I've made will suit you.
C Of course you could do any of these things with a group of friends as well.
D That's something you can do on your own.
E I do both of these things with my family out in the countryside.

Does the email read better with or without the extra sentences? Why?

6 In pairs, look at the letter and email again and choose the correct answer.

The style of the letter and email is usually (1) *formal / informal*. They are usually written to a (2) *friend / stranger*. This means that you (3) *will / won't* find short forms of the verbs in them.

You (4) *do / don't* need to begin your reply with some news about yourself and your family. There will (5) *always / usually* be several questions to answer. You can finish your letter or email by (6) *offering more help if necessary / wishing someone luck*. You (7) *don't need to / should* check your reply to make sure you have given a complete answer. You have to write (8) *more / less* than 200 words.

7 Tick the best ways to start and end an informal letter or email.

Start: Dear ☐ Hello ☐ Hi ☐
Finish: All the best ☐ Best wishes ☐
Good luck with everything ☐ Love ☐
Hope that helps ☐ Yours ☐
With kind regards ☐

Exam task

8 Read the letter and email below with your partner, and decide what advice you could give to Sarah and Sam.

9 Write an answer to either the letter or the email.

Remember to:
- make sure you understand the whole situation
- plan your letter or email before you begin
- write in an appropriate style
- begin and end appropriately
- write 140–190 words.

A

You have received a letter from your English-speaking pen friend.

> My German pen friend has asked me to go and stay with her for two weeks in the school holidays, but my parents won't allow me to go. Do you think it's a good idea? What can I do to persuade them to let me go? Please give me some suggestions!
>
> Thanks,
>
> Sarah

Write your **letter**.

B

You have received an email from your English-speaking friend.

> Help! I've got a difficult decision to make. I've just got into my school football team, so there'll be lots of matches to play on a Saturday. But I've also just got a place in a local orchestra for young people, and all the concerts they do are also on a Saturday. I can't do both, so which shall I choose?
>
> Write soon.
>
> Best wishes, Sam

Write your **email**.

W *See pages 89-90*

5 Learning
READING AND USE OF ENGLISH

Part 7

1 Some of the words below have similar meanings. Work in pairs. Choose one word to match each of the dictionary definitions.

> adventurous   capable   cheerful
> communicative   competitive   creative
> decisive   easygoing   energetic
> sympathetic   thorough

1 understanding and caring about other people's feelings
2 willing to talk to people and give them information
3 willing to try new, difficult and often exciting things
4 wanting very much to win or be more successful than others
5 having imagination or original ideas
6 able to do things effectively and skilfully and achieve results

2 Look at these photos. Which jobs are shown?

3 What kind of personality do you need in order to be good at different jobs? For each of the photos, choose some of the adjectives in Exercise 1.

What else is important for these jobs? Think of some more adjectives for each photo.

4 If you could choose one of the careers in the photos, which one would you choose? Which career would you never choose and why?

Exam task

You are going to read a magazine article about talented young people. For questions 1–10, choose from the people (**A–D**). The people may be chosen more than once.

> **Exam tip**
>
> Read text A, go through the questions and find all the A answers. Repeat for texts B–D. Finally, go back and look for any missing answers.

Which person

combined two interests into a possible career?	1
wants to offer support to others in a similar situation?	2
knows it will be necessary to keep their knowledge up to date?	3
was unsure of the extent of their ability at one stage?	4
has always used their talent to help them escape from daily life?	5
came to a sudden decision about what they wanted to do as a job?	6
admires others because of their characteristics rather than their achievements?	7
was unaware that something was possible until it was pointed out?	8
thinks it is an advantage to stand out from others when young?	9
says they come across successful people who look down on others?	10

My Ambition

We interviewed four talented young people who are already on the way to successful careers.

A Laura

Laura Stanley is only 15 and has already produced an impressive collection of poems and short stories. Her aunt is a writer and used to read the stories Laura wrote when young. Laura really looked up to her aunt and in return she received a lot of encouragement. But she also used to sing solos in the school choir and was an accomplished artist and dancer. For a long time she thought she might follow one of those paths as a career, as at the time she didn't really know whether she was good enough at writing. But in the end she has decided that writing is what she loves. 'I know that other kids think I'm weird sometimes because I'd rather be writing than out doing things but it's no bad thing to be a bit different at this stage. You don't get anywhere unless you're different.'

B Haruki

Haruki Kato is a highly dedicated young sculptor. At the age of 16, he has already had his work displayed in galleries and won several competitions. He says he's always sculpted: 'For me, it's a way of losing myself in a fantasy world, of cutting everything else out.' He says he's inspired not by successful artists, but by anyone who is driven and determined to get where they want. 'I have a lot of people around me who have helped me and made sure I improve and grow as an artist. In the future, I'd like to do the same for children like me who have a talent but need encouragement so they don't give up. If I weren't studying for exams, I'd spend some of my time teaching them now.'

C Elena

Elena Mancini is a 17-year-old make-up artist with plans for the future. She's already working in local theatres and has even helped on a film set. 'People in our village have always put on plays and my mum does all the make-up. I used to beg her to let me help her and she put up with me getting in her way. If she had stopped me from helping, I wouldn't have found out how much I enjoy doing make-up. For ages though, I didn't realise that you could do this as a job, so I tried to make myself enjoy science as my parents are both scientists. But then a friend told me about a course you can do.' Elena knows it's a demanding job. 'If I want to do well, I'll have to work very hard. The make-up world is always changing, so it's necessary to be constantly learning new techniques.'

D Joel

Joel Bailey, who is 15, wants to be a music journalist and he has already had some interviews published in music magazines. 'For ages, I really didn't know what I wanted to do after school. But I'm a big fan of rock music and I read all the music magazines when I can get hold of them. I enjoy writing as well, and one day I just came up with the idea that I could be a journalist and specialise in music. So I started writing articles and sending them off to magazines. Some I didn't even get paid for, but I didn't mind, because if you want to succeed in any business, you have to get recognised and learn your skills. The only thing I don't like about the music business is that you come across some people who are very arrogant because they feel they are better than the rest of us.'

5 READING AND USE OF ENGLISH

Part 1

Vocabulary – Phrasal verbs

1 In Reading and Use of English Part 1 you often need to choose which phrasal verb fits into a gap. Look back at the questions and texts on pages 38 and 39 and underline these verbs.

point out (Q8)   stand out (Q9)   look down on (Q10)   look up to (A)
give up (B)   put up with (C)   come up with (D)   come across (D)

2 It is often possible to guess the meaning of phrasal verbs from the words around them, even if you haven't seen them before. Match the phrasal verbs in Exercise 1 with these meanings.

1 think of (an idea or suggestion)
2 accept a difficult or unpleasant situation
3 meet someone or find something by chance
4 stop doing something
5 tell someone something
6 think someone is less important than you
7 admire or respect someone
8 be better than other similar things or people

> **Exam tip**
>
> Questions 1, 2 and 5 in the Exam task test phrasal verbs. You will find more practice of these verbs in the Workbook.

Exam task

For questions 1–8, read the text below and decide which answer (A, B, C or D) best fits each gap. There is an example at the beginning (0).

How my dream came true!

I was born in Pakistan, a country with a vivid history and (0) ..D.. traditions. Despite loving my country, as a child I decided I wanted to go and live and study in the USA, so I would have to (1) .... a way of persuading my family to move there. Then, when I was fourteen and had almost given (2) .... the idea, my father (3) .... announced that we were actually moving there! I quickly (4) .... to the American way of life because I'd learnt a lot about the country from the films and books I'd (5) .... and many things seemed (6) .... to me. In Pakistan they often say that a person should be judged not (7) .... by his past achievements but also by his dreams. I'm seventeen now and my ambition is to become a doctor and to go back to work in Pakistan. I'm sure that if I work hard, I will have no difficulty in (8) .... that goal.

0	A	elderly	B	antique	C	past	D	ancient
1	A	go over	B	come down with	C	come up with	D	go through
2	A	up	B	away	C	back	D	out
3	A	carelessly	B	unexpectedly	C	accidentally	D	undoubtedly
4	A	suited	B	altered	C	matched	D	adapted
5	A	kept to	B	come across	C	gone into	D	put up with
6	A	common	B	usual	C	familiar	D	frequent
7	A	quite	B	much	C	even	D	only
8	A	achieving	B	obtaining	C	performing	D	acquiring

Part 4

Grammar – Conditionals G *See page 82*

3 Complete these conditional sentences, then check your answers with the reading texts on page 39.

1. If I weren't studying for exams, I .... some of my time teaching them now.
2. If she had stopped me from helping, I .... how much I enjoy doing make-up.
3. If I want to do well, I .... work very hard.
4. If you want to succeed in any business, you .... get recognised.

4 Which sentence in Exercise 3 is about:

a past events which can't be changed?
b something which is likely in the future?
c something which is impossible or unlikely?
d something which is a general statement of fact?

5 Read the examples and then complete the definitions below with the underlined expressions.

You can go to the beach <u>providing (that) / provided (that)</u> you finish your homework.
Tom will come swimming <u>as/so long as</u> he finishes his homework in time.
I'll bring my coat <u>in case</u> it rains.
We'll go to the beach <u>unless</u> it rains.

1. .... means the same as *except if*.
2. .... means *because it's possible something might happen*.
3. .... and .... mean the same as *only if* or *on condition that*.

6 Choose the correct expression in these sentences.

1. I'll come to the film *unless / as long as* there's a match on TV I want to watch.
2. I won't come to the film *if / unless* there's a match on TV I want to watch.
3. Take some money *unless / in case* you need to get the bus home.
4. I'll lend you some money *in case / so long as* you give it back tomorrow.

Exam task

For questions 1–6, complete the second sentence so it has a similar meaning to the first sentence, using the word given. Do not change the word given. You must use between two and five words, including the word given.

> **Exam tip ›**
>
> The sentence you write needs to include the word in capitals and to be grammatically correct. It must also have the same meaning as the first sentence.

0 I suddenly thought of how I could persuade my mum to let me go on the trip.
CAME
I suddenly *came up with a* way of persuading my mum to let me go on the trip.

1 I don't think we'll be chosen for the team because we're not practising enough.
UNLESS
We won't be chosen for the team .... more.

2 I'll come to the party if you let my sister come too.
PROVIDED
I'll come to the party .... allowed to come too.

3 The museum might not have a café so we need to take a packed lunch.
CASE
We need to take a packed lunch .... a café in the museum.

4 I regret not having done any revision, but I didn't know the test was today.
HAVE
If I had known the test was today, I .... revision.

5 I can't wait to find out what you've bought me for my birthday.
FORWARD
I'm really .... out what you've bought me for my birthday.

6 To be good at a sport, you have to do several hours of practice every day.
NEED
If you want to be good at a sport, you .... several hours every day.

5 LISTENING

Education

Part 2

1 Work in pairs. Make sentences about yourself with some of these words.

attend ☐   primary school ☐   head ☐   secondary school ☐   state ☐
comprehensive ☐   streamed ☐   set ☐   uniform ☐   sports kit ☐   lessons ☐
pupils ☐   playing fields ☐   canteen ☐   laboratories ☐   library ☐
swimming pool ☐   teacher ☐   classes ☐   timetable ☐   homework ☐   rules ☐

2 🔊 14 Now listen to Anna, an English girl, talking about her education. Tick (✔) the words from Exercise 1 she uses. They are listed in order.

3 Anna used these words on the recording. Match the underlined words in the sentences in Exercise 4 with a word below which has the same meaning.

   attended   catching   highest group   put on

4 🔊 14 Now listen to the recording again and complete the gaps with one or two words.

   1 Anna <u>went to</u> a .... school very close to her home.
   2 Anna is in the <u>top set</u> for ....
   3 Anna had to <u>wear</u> a white polo shirt and .... for sports lessons.
   4 Anna found <u>getting</u> the .... difficult because she wasn't used to it.

5 Work in groups of three or four to answer these questions.

   1 Anna has attended state schools. Is the school you are at a state school or a private one?
   2 Anna's secondary school is *comprehensive* (anyone can go to it). Do children have to take an exam to get a place in your school or can anyone go?
   3 Subjects at Anna's school are *streamed*. Are children at your school divided into groups or sets for different subjects according to their ability? Is this a good idea?
   4 Anna's school has good *facilities*, like playing fields and a canteen. Are the facilities at your school good?

Exam tip

The words you hear before (or occasionally after) you hear the answer in the recording will be similar in meaning to the words in the question, but the words themselves may not be the same.

6 Work in pairs. Discuss these questions about educational visits.

What is an educational visit? What sort of places do you go to on an educational visit? Have you been on any educational visits with your class/school? Where did you go?

7 You are going to hear a boy talking about a class educational visit. Look at the photos. What do you think he saw there? Write down five words you think you might hear in the talk.

8 Now look at the underlined words in the Exam task below. Match them with words in the box with the same meaning. You will hear these words in the recording.

| amazed   building   built   came to a close   defended |
| described   didn't appear   hard   not far from   press |

Exam task

🔘 15 You will hear a student called Max talking about his visit to the Aeroseum in Gothenberg, Sweden. For questions 1–10, complete the sentences with a word or short phrase.

VISIT TO THE AEROSEUM

The museum is built <u>very close to</u> an old (1) .... and situated in some underground shelters.

During the <u>construction</u> of the shelters, a lot of (2) .... had to be moved.

The shelters <u>could not be found</u> on (3) .... after they were built, so for years no one knew about them.

To enter the museum, you have to <u>push</u> a (4) .... by the main doors.

The main doors were made very thick so they <u>could protect</u> everything from (5) ....

Max was <u>surprised</u> to see some (6) .... which looked very modern just inside the museum.

Max thought the pilot would have found the (7) .... of the cockpit <u>difficult</u> to deal with.

Max preferred listening to a volunteer who <u>talked about</u> (8) .... and flying planes.

Max enjoyed watching some people covering a wing <u>made</u> of (9) ....

Max's visit <u>ended</u> in the (10) .... room.

9 Work in pairs. Did you get all the answers right? If not, what mistakes did you make?

A I spelled the word wrong. Questions ....
B I wrote the wrong answer. Questions ....
C I got lost and missed the answer. Questions ....

Exam tip

The first possible answer you hear will not necessarily be the correct one. Some words are there to distract you!

5 SPEAKING

Vocabulary – School subjects

1 Tick (✔) the subjects you are studying, then compare with a partner.

English ☐   other foreign languages ☐
my own language and literature ☐
maths ☐   science ☐   history ☐
geography ☐   IT ☐   sport ☐
art ☐   music ☐   drama ☐
other subjects: ....

2 Tell your partner which of the subjects in Exercise 1 you like best. Use reasons a–e to explain why.

a I'm good at it.
b The teacher's great.
c It's an interesting subject.
d It'll be useful.
e Other: ....

Part 1

3 Match the speech bubbles with the questions, then, in pairs, ask and answer them. Remember to add some extra information.

A I'd love to learn Chinese if I could.

B I hope to pass all my exams and go to university.

C I'd like to be a scientist if I get good grades.

D How to sit still!

Ambitions and achievements
1 What job would you like to do when you grow up?
2 What do you expect to achieve in the next five years?

Education
3 What was the most important thing you learned at primary school?
4 Is there a new subject you'd really like to study?

Part 2

4 Work in pairs and do the task below.

Candidate A: Look at photographs 1 and 2. Compare them and answer the question. Tell your answer to Candidate B. Use these phrases if you are not sure about what you see in the photos: *it may/might/could be a ... it looks like a ... it's similar to a ... it's a sort of ...*
Candidate B: When Candidate A has finished, discuss together which lesson you would prefer to do and why. Give reasons. Here are some phrases you can use:
I'd rather ... because it's more interesting. It's good to learn something new. I'd rather be outside. I don't like/enjoy doing ... because ...

> **Exam tip**
> Don't worry if you don't know a particular word, or if you are unsure what you can see in the photographs! Keep talking and make intelligent guesses using the phrases above.

What might pupils learn by doing these different subjects at school?

What do you think the pupils will learn on their visits?

Exam task

Now do the same with photographs 3 and 4. Candidate B should start. Use the phrases in Exercise 4 to help you. When Candidate B has finished, discuss which of the visits you would prefer to go on and why.

5 WRITING

Part 2: Set text

Which book are you reading? Write the title and the name of the author here.

....

Work in pairs.

1 Who are the main characters? Make a list and describe them briefly.
2 Write a brief description (50–70 words) of what happens in the book.
3 What are the main events in the book? Write a list and put the events in the correct order.
4 Now read these exam questions on the set text. They can be in the form of essays, articles, letters/emails or reviews. Your teacher will tell you how to complete each question.

Essay

> Your English class has had a discussion about [book]. Now your teacher has given you this essay for homework:
>
> > Is [name] the hero/heroine of [book]? Describe him/her and say what he or she does in the book that is courageous.
>
> Write your **essay**.

Article

> You have seen this announcement in an English-language magazine for young people.
>
> > **Articles wanted**
> > **A brilliant ending to a book!**
> > How does [book] end? Why did you think it was so good?
> > Write and tell us. The best articles will be published in the magazine.
>
> Write your **article** about the ending of the book.

Letter/email

> You have received a letter from your English-speaking friend.
>
> > I've just finished reading [book]. I know you've read it too. I didn't like [name] at all, because I thought he/she behaved very badly. What did you think about him/her?
> > Write and tell me!
> > Anya
>
> Write your **letter**.

Review

> Your English class has had a discussion about [book]. Now your teacher has asked you to write a review for the school magazine explaining what you found interesting about [book], what you disliked about it and whether you would recommend it to other students of your age.
>
> Write your **review**.

5 Your teacher will divide you into groups. Work in pairs and plan your answer to one of the questions.

Exam task

Write your answer to one of the questions for homework, using the plan you made in class.
Remember you have 30 minutes to write 140–190 words, and 5 minutes for checking your work.

W *See pages 91-92*

6 Natural world
LISTENING

Environment and weather

Part 4

1 Work in pairs. Which photo shows these things, A, B, C or D? (Some may be in more than one photo.)

| bushes   grass   grey sky   lakes   mountains |
| pine trees   rocks   snow and ice   sunshine   volcanoes |

2 Now match the photos with these countries. What helped you to decide?

| Australia   Cameroon   Canada   Iceland |

3 🔊 16 You will hear three teenagers each talking about the weather and environment in one of the countries above. Which country does each speaker talk about?

Speaker 1 ....   Speaker 2 ....   Speaker 3 ....

Which words gave you the answer?

4 🔊 16 Listen again and make a list of the adjectives, nouns and expressions the speakers use to describe the weather.

Adjectives	Nouns	Expressions
mild	*sunshine*	*temperatures below zero*

5 Tick (✔) the words and expressions that can be used about your country. In pairs, talk about the weather in your country. What is your favourite time of year? Why?

6 Which countries in the box have the problems below? Choose one or two for each problem. Work in pairs or small groups. You can find the information on the internet or in a book if you need to.

> Bangladesh   Brazil   Italy   Jamaica
> Saudi Arabia   Spain   Switzerland
> the USA

forests disappearing ...... *Brazil* ....
volcanoes erupting ....
industrial pollution ....
rivers drying up ....
lack of rain ....
flooding ....
hurricanes ....
ice melting ....

Do you have any of these problems in your country? What can be done about them?

Grammar – Countable and uncountable nouns G *See page 83*

7 *River* is a countable noun and *pollution* is an uncountable noun. Answer these questions about countable and uncountable nouns.

   1 Which kind of noun can be singular or plural?
   2 Which kind of noun cannot be plural and takes a singular verb?

8 Write the nouns from Exercises 1, 4 and 6 in the correct list.

Countable	Uncountable
river	pollution

Exam task

> **Exam tip**
>
> If you find a question difficult, listen for words which tell you which of the possible answers are wrong. This will make it easier to choose the correct one.

🔊 17 You will hear a boy called Tim talking about a school project he has done on the environment. For questions 1–7, choose the best answer (A, B or C).

1 Why did Tim choose to do a project on the environment?
   A His family persuaded him to take part.
   B He wanted to take positive action.
   C He was interested in the scientific issues.

2 What change has Tim made in his travel habits?
   A He walks to school rather than taking the bus.
   B He catches the bus to school rather than travelling by car.
   C He cycles to school instead of getting a lift.

3 What suggestion will Tim make about paper use at school?
   A Students should use only paper that has been recycled.
   B Students should avoid using paper when submitting work.
   C Students should use both sides of paper whenever possible.

4 What improvement does Tim propose for the school cafeteria?
   A getting rid of drinks machines
   B making the menu vegetarian
   C purchasing food grown locally

5 Tim thinks that all young people should
   A study in natural light whenever possible.
   B turn off electrical equipment they're not using.
   C try to avoid using air conditioning.

6 What does Tim say about using water?
   A Everyone can take steps to reduce water waste.
   B An international solution is needed for water shortages.
   C Some people refuse to try and save water.

7 What does Tim believe families should do when shopping?
   A avoid buying expensive ready meals
   B refuse to pay for unnecessary plastic bags
   C reduce the amount of packaged food they buy

9 Now your teacher will show you what Tim said. In pairs, look at the recording script for each question, and underline the words that give you the answer. Then highlight the words that show you the other answers are wrong.

> **Exam tip**
>
> The answers will be in the same order as the questions, so keep listening even if you miss an answer.

6 SPEAKING

Part 3

1 Your school is thinking of things students can do to improve and protect the environment. Look at the suggestions below. Make some notes. For each suggestion think about:
   - what you could do in your school
   - how successful it might be

- growing plants
- saving electricity
- recycling
- using less water
- using less plastic

How could students in your school protect the environment by doing these things?

2 In Speaking Part 3, the examiner gives you a task with a question and some suggestions. You have a discussion about the suggestions and then you are asked to make a decision. Here are some useful expressions. Write A, D, C or S next to each one for Agree, Disagree, make a Comment, make a Suggestion.

1 I don't really think that's a good idea.
2 Absolutely.
3 We all know we shouldn't drop litter.
4 We could tell everyone to turn off their computers at the end of the lesson.
5 I don't think turning the heating down would go down well with students here.
6 I'm with you on that.
7 That's not what I think, I'm afraid.
8 What about getting recycling bins in the canteen?

Exam task

Now practise doing the task in Exercise 1 with your partner. Talk about the question and the suggestions for about two minutes. Then spend about a minute talking about this question.

Which two suggestions would be most successful?

> **Exam tip**
>
> Start speaking straight away so you use the time allowed. Cooperate with your partner and ask him/her to respond, e.g. *What do you think? Do you agree? And you?*

Part 4

Exam task

The examiner will ask you some general questions related to Part 3. You have four minutes to complete Part 4 in the exam. Take it in turns to ask and answer the questions below with your partner.

- Do you think your school is environmentally friendly? Why? / Why not?
- Do you think young people care about the environment more than older people? Why? / Why not?
- Are young people taught enough about the environment at school? Should there be any changes?
- Does the media do enough to make young people aware of environmental problems?
- Do people use cars too much instead of walking or cycling? Why is this a problem?

6 WRITING

Part 2: Article

1 You may be asked to write an article on a very wide range of subjects. You don't always have to be very serious, but you do need to get the reader's attention and keep it. Which of these strategies will help you to do this?

1. asking questions to involve the reader
2. making an amusing comment
3. using long and complicated words
4. finishing in a memorable way
5. making lots of comparisons
6. giving personal examples

2 This article was written for a school magazine. Read it and find examples of the helpful strategies in Exercise 1. Highlight them in different colours.

What I do to be 'green' at home and at school

We all have to do something to help the environment, don't we? I'm only 14 though, so there's no way I personally can do anything about the really big problems, like climate change, is there?

However, I can make sure I live my own life in a green way. It is about making little changes which make a big difference. At home that means not taking baths, because they use too much hot water. (Don't worry, I still take showers!) I turn off the lights and heating in my room when I leave, so I don't waste electricity. I'm very green when it comes to transport too, because I walk everywhere. When I go out with my family we often take the train rather than the car, especially if we want to go into the city, and also it's quicker and parking is expensive.

At school, I help to collect and recycle all the rubbish. That involves collecting everything from the cafeteria. Our head teacher has also decided to turn the central heating on a month later than usual. It's OK, I've put my jumper on!

So I can honestly say that I'm as green as I can be. Are you?

3 Compare your answers with a partner and then answer these questions.

Is this article written in a formal or informal style? Is this appropriate? Why? Can you think of any different ways to end the article?

4 Here is part of another article. Complete the main paragraph with the underlined words and phrases in the article in Exercise 2. Use each only once.

My favourite time of year

Why do I love July? Most of all (1) .... school has finished and that (2) .... going to the beach with my friends, relaxing on the warm sand, swimming and snorkelling. (3) .... eating out, we often have lunch in a little restaurant on the beach, (4) .... we want to meet my aunt and my cousins. We always spend the evenings there too; when it's warm, the stars are shining and the music is playing, it's absolute magic. Wouldn't anyone love this experience? For me summer (5) .... not having any stress or pressure, relaxing and enjoying the sunshine. (6) .... we sometimes have to travel miles to visit relations who I hardly know.

5 Now write out the article, giving it a good introduction and a memorable ending. Try to put a question in the introduction, and add an amusing comment to the main paragraph.

Exam task

Do one of the following tasks for homework (140–190 words).

A Your English teacher has asked you to write an article for the school magazine with the title: *What I love and hate about the weather in my country.*

B You have seen this announcement on an international website:

Articles wanted!
Do you have problems with the environment and pollution in your country?
Write and tell us about them, **and** say whether you think these problems can be solved.
The best articles will be posted on the website next month.

Write your **article**.
Remember to:
- give your article a title.
- begin with an interesting introduction.
- involve your reader with questions.
- use your own knowledge and experience.
- try to end it in an amusing or interesting way.

W *See pages 90-91*

6 READING AND USE OF ENGLISH

Part 6

1 Work in pairs. What are these animals and where can you find them?

2 In what ways are these animals different from each other? Think about where they live, what they look like and what they eat. Use a dictionary to help you if necessary.

> A lives in the jungle but C lives in the ocean.

> And B lives on grassland, in Africa, I think.

3 Do the three animals have anything in common? If so, what?

4 Read this short text and the sentences which follow. Underline the differences between the three sentences. Which sentence fits best in the gap?

> Elephants have huge ears which are capable of detecting all kinds of noises which a human cannot hear. .... There is a wide range of these that can travel huge distances and are picked up not just by other elephants' ears but also by the soles of their feet.

A Because of this, the sounds they produce are even more impressive.
B Therefore, the sounds they produce are even more impressive.
C The sounds they produce, however, are even more impressive.

Exam tip

Words and expressions like *however*, *though*, *because of this* and *therefore* help you decide if a sentence follows the argument in a text and fits in a gap. Read before and after the gap.

Exam task

You are going to read an article about the 'singing' of humpback whales. Six sentences have been removed from the article. Choose from the sentences A–G the one which fits each gap (1–6). There is one extra sentence that you do not need to use.

Even humpback whales have hit songs!

The fact that male humpback whales sing long, sweet melodies has been known for many years. However, a new finding suggests that some melodies become so popular that they are sung by whales all over the world!

Before we look further into this exciting discovery, here is a bit of background about the tunes sung by these mammals. Unlike the songs released as records by humans, which last for three or four minutes, these soulful whale songs last for ten to twenty minutes. **1** ▢ Scientists are not sure whether they sing to attract females or to ward off competitors, but apparently once they begin, the mammals sing the same song over and over, for 24 hours at a time.

Also, they 'release' a new song every year which can be totally original. **2** ▢ What is really interesting, though, about this 'song of the year' is that while scientists have known for some time that it is sung by the entire population of male whales that live in one group (known as a pod), they recently discovered that it was also 'downloaded' by whales that lived in other areas of the world.

This new research was conducted by University of Queensland biologists Ellen Garland and Michael Noad, who recorded songs from six different Pacific whale populations over a number of years. What they observed is amazing. In almost every case, the annual songs originated from a pod of humpback whales off Australia's eastern coast. **3** ▢

One such song became such a super hit that it travelled all the way to the Atlantic! Since they don't have iTunes or iPods, this process takes about two years. The scientists are not yet sure whether the songs were passed on by humpbacks who moved from one pod to another, or were shared by the different populations when they met while they were migrating from one area to another. **4** ▢ This is something that has never been observed before in the animal kingdom and in this respect they are very similar to humans.

Since they are amongst the largest species of whales, humpbacks are easy to spot. **5** ▢ These incredible mammals can dive for up to 45 minutes, reach depths of 180 metres and see underwater for more than 120 metres. They can blow bubbles from their blowholes on the top of their heads at speeds exceeding 450 kilometres per hour and have lungs large enough to hold nearly 10,000 litres of air.

6 ▢ Their famous songs, which can be heard for over 160 kilometres, are 'sung' by blowing air through their blowholes. The one sad part is that there are currently only about 10,000 of these wonderful creatures left.

A Their most amazing feature, though, is that they have no vocal cords.
B However, the finding is considered very important, because it confirms that whales exchange their culture with each other.
C And they are not just random noises, but are made of actual themes that keep repeating and developing.
D More often than not though, it is actually a remix of a previous one.
E Therefore they appeared to stay still for some time in one geographical location while they did this.
F This is also thanks to the unique markings on the underside of their tail.
G The same song would move from group to group, until it was being sung by whales about 4,000 miles away.

5 Work in pairs to discuss the following.

1 When you have finished the task, compare your answers with a partner. If you disagree on an answer, look at the question again, and see if you can work out who is right.
2 What will you do in the exam if you are unable to answer a question?
3 What is the writer comparing the whales to in this text? Why?

6 READING AND USE OF ENGLISH

Part 2

Grammar – Articles G *See page 83*

1 Put the correct words into the rules about articles.

> a   an   the   no article

We use …
1 .... or .... with singular countable nouns that introduce a new item of information.
2 .... with countable and uncountable nouns, when the item has been mentioned before.
3 .... + noun when the speaker and listener both know what they are talking about.
4 .... with uncountable and plural countable nouns when we talk about things in a general sense.
5 .... with the names of most buildings, cities, countries, lakes, towns, villages and mountains.
6 .... with the names of certain countries (with the word *Kingdom*, *Republic* or *State*), regions, deserts, mountain ranges, oceans, rivers and seas.

2 Which of these place names need *the* before them? Write them next to the correct heading.

> Amazon   Atlantic Ocean   California
> Czech Republic   Far East   Himalayas
> Italy   Lake Como   London   north of England
> Sahara   South America   Thames
> United Kingdom   United States

Oceans, seas and rivers: *the* ....
Regions: *the* ....
Countries: *the* ....
Deserts and mountain ranges: *the* ....

Add some more examples to the lists if you can.

3 👁 Complete these sentences with *a* or *the*.

1 I heard .... strange noise coming from downstairs in .... kitchen.
2 Julie wanted .... cold drink but there were no drinks left in .... fridge.
3 We took .... taxi to .... airport because we had so much luggage.
4 They learned .... words of .... new song in class yesterday.
5 I really enjoyed reading .... book you lent me.

4 Which sentences need *the* and which need no article? Complete them with *the* or leave a gap.

1 All the pupils at my school study .... geography.
2 We studied .... geography of India in class yesterday.
3 I gave my sister .... money I owed her.
4 My grandparents say that .... money doesn't always make you happy.

5 Complete the text with *a*, *an*, *the* or leave a gap for no article.

Some interesting facts about the weather and climate

- Recent increases in temperatures across **(1)** .... world have been linked to human activity, such as **(2)** .... burning of fossil fuels like **(3)** .... oil and coal. Global warming has become **(4)** .... important issue for governments everywhere as they try to find **(5)** .... way to deal with **(6)** .... effects of climate change.

- The hottest temperature ever recorded was 57.8 °C in **(7)** .... Libya in September 1922. **(8)** .... coldest was at Vostok Station in **(9)** .... Antarctica in July 1983. It was – 89.2 °C!

- The highest rainfall ever recorded in 24 hours was 182.5 cm in La Réunion, during **(10)** .... Hurricane Denise in January 1966. The most rainfall ever recorded in one year was 25.4 m in **(11)** .... India.

- The highest snowfall ever recorded in **(12)** .... one-year period was 31.1 m in **(13)** .... Washington State, in 1972.

- **(14)** .... USA also has more tornadoes than any other country, averaging around 1200 each year.

- **(15)** .... water covers 70% of **(16)** .... Earth's surface, the three largest oceans being **(17)** .... Pacific, **(18)** .... Atlantic and **(19)** .... Indian Ocean. The longest river in the world is **(20)** .... Nile, which is 6,650 km in length.

52 UNIT 6 READING AND USE OF ENGLISH

Grammar – so and such (a/an) See page 83

6 Complete the sentences with *so* or *such*.

1 The Siberian tiger is ………………… a rare animal that few people have seen one.
2 The recycling campaign was ………………… well organised that everyone took part.
3 The students responded with ………………… enthusiasm to the idea of 'adopting' an animal at the zoo that the teacher organised it at once.
4 The talk about the rainforest was attended by ………………… a lot of people that there weren't enough chairs.
5 Plans to build a new motorway were dropped because ………………… many people objected.
6 The deer ran away ………………… rapidly that the lion couldn't catch it.

Now complete the rules.

We use ………………… with nouns (with or without an adjective) and the expression *a lot (of)*.
We use ………………… with an adjective or adverb and the words *many*, *much* and *few*.

too and enough

7 Write a sentence about each cartoon using *too* or *enough* and one of these words.

| big   food   money   steep |

Exam task

> **Exam tip**
>
> Write your answers in the gaps, then read the text to make sure it makes sense before you transfer your answers to the answer sheet.

For questions 1–8, read the text below and think of the word which best fits each gap. Use only one word in each gap. There is an example at the beginning (0).

Lala the Penguin

You might think all penguins live somewhere really cold **(0)** *like* ………… Antarctica, but not Lala. This fourteen-year-old King Penguin not **(1)** ………………… lives in Japan, but is also a household pet.

Lala's path to domestic life began about ten years **(2)** ………………… , after he was accidentally caught in a fisherman's net. He was **(3)** ………………… sick to swim away, so he was rescued and nursed back to health by a family. However, **(4)** ………………… they tried to return him to the water, Lala refused to leave, so **(5)** ………………… family decided to adopt him instead and installed him in a giant room with air-conditioning.

If **(6)** ………………… is one thing Lala likes more than this cool and comfortable accommodation, it is his daily shopping trip to town. His first and only stop is at the local fish store, **(7)** ………………… he buys two fish and puts them in his penguin-shaped backpack. He is **(8)** ………………… familiar to local people now that nobody takes any notice!

8 Check your answers with a partner. If you disagree, explain to each other why your answer is right or wrong.

7 People and style
LISTENING

Part 3

Shopping and fashion

1 Work in pairs. Choose three of the adjectives and expressions to describe the clothes in each photo.

casual   colourful   comfortable   cool
designer clothes   elegant
everyday   expensive-looking   formal
individual   outrageous   second-hand
smart   sports clothes   stylish
unfashionable   vintage   well-designed

2 Discuss these questions in a group.
1 Do you ever dress like the people in the photographs? When?
2 What are your favourite clothes?
3 Do you prefer to wear the same clothes as your friends?
4 Can you tell someone's personality from their clothes?

3 🎧 18 Listen to one of the people in the photos. In pairs, answer these questions.
1 Which person is speaking?
2 Is he/she like you?
3 Do you know anyone like this?

4 🎧 18 The expressions below are different from those the speaker uses but they have a similar meaning. Try to remember and write some of the words she uses. Then listen again and write the rest.

1 be passionate about
2 staying in touch with
3 look different
4 slightly shocking
5 fairly typical
6 look good on me
7 becomes unfashionable
8 get rid of
9 become fashionable again
10 be very rich
11 draw attention to yourself
12 clothes by particular designers

Exam task

Exam tip >

You need to listen for words and expressions with similar meanings to those in the questions.

🎧 19 You will hear five people talking about shopping for clothes. For questions 1–5, choose from the list (A–H) what each speaker says. Use the letters only once. There are three extra letters which you do not need to use.

A I prefer certain colours.
B I am passionate about the latest fashions.
C I try to stand out from everyone else.
D My tastes change quickly.
E I know what styles suit me.
F I dress in the same way as my friends.
G I spend a lot on clothes.
H I like to look smart.

Speaker 1 ☐
Speaker 2 ☐
Speaker 3 ☐
Speaker 4 ☐
Speaker 5 ☐

7 SPEAKING

Part 1

1 🎧 20 Listen to two students answering some Part 1 questions and write down what they like and dislike.

	Like	Dislike	Neither like nor dislike
Sofia			
Daniel			

2 🎧 20 Listen again and complete the phrases they use.

Like	Dislike	Neither like nor dislike
I'm .... music. I .... singing. I'm .... football, of course. I .... going to see them ... I'm .... skiing. History and geography are	I'm .... playing football myself. I .... playing other sports very much. I'm .... going to the mountains in the summer. I .... going for long walks.	Well, English is OK but it's .... I .... doing science.

Exam task

Work in pairs to ask and answer the questions below. If your partner doesn't have much to say, use the questions in brackets to help.

> **Exam tip**
>
> The examiner will ask you some questions about your everyday life, your free time and your school. This will include some questions about what you like.

- Do you prefer watching sports to playing them? (Why?)
- Do you enjoy watching TV? (Tell me about a programme you have watched recently.)
- Do you enjoy reading books? (What kind of books do you like? / Why don't you enjoy reading books?)
- What do you like doing on holiday? (Why do you enjoy it?)

Grammar – Verbs and expressions followed by *to-* infinitive or *-ing* form

G *See page 84*

3 Sofia and Daniel used these verbs and expressions. Which ones are followed by a *to-* infinitive and which by the *-ing* form of the verb? Put them by the correct heading.

> attempt   can't bear   don't mind
> enjoy   hope   be interested in
> be keen on   like   love   prefer
> want   would like   would prefer

to- infinitive	
-ing form	
either *to-* infinitive or *-ing* form	

4 👁 Exam candidates often make mistakes with verb forms. Choose the correct form in these sentences and put any new verbs into the table in Exercise 3.

1 If you agree *coming / to come*, just bring some cold cola, because it'll be hot.
2 I look forward to *seeing / see* you at the airport.
3 I hope *see / to see* you on Monday!
4 Would you like *come / to come* to visit me?
5 I would prefer *going / to go* to a film rather than watch TV.
6 I suggested *going / to go* for a walk along the beach.
7 I cannot imagine *to live / living* in a small village.
8 Your parents don't want you *go / to go* somewhere dangerous.
9 I prefer *to buy / buy* clothes by myself and with my own money.
10 I love *playing / play* tennis in the school team.

Part 2

5 These photos show four different ways of shopping. Which of the ways do you prefer?

6 **21** Listen to Adam, a student, talking in a speaking exam. Which of the photos has Adam been given? Tick (✔) the ideas below which he mentions.

Advantages

lots of choice ☐   more unusual stuff for sale ☐
other facilities ☐   compare prices ☐   convenient ☐
you can try clothes on ☐   latest fashions ☐   more fun ☐

Disadvantages

quite traditional ☐   too crowded ☐
not much for teenagers ☐   bad quality ☐
can't try things on ☐   wait for the post ☐

7 Complete the expressions Adam used when he didn't know what to say.

1 Mmm, ... me ....
2 .... me .... for a ....
3 Not .... would .... but I think ...

> **Exam tip**
>
> When you need to think, say something in English to give yourself time.

8 Work in pairs. Write down other things you could say about the photographs Adam talked about.

9 Now look at the other two photographs. Can you use the same ideas to talk about these photos? Try to think of some more ideas and write them down.

Exam task

Work in pairs. Choose two photographs each and compare them. Say what the advantages are of shopping in these ways. Time yourselves and talk for one minute each.

Here are some words you can use to connect your ideas about the photos:

| whereas   on the other hand |
| the difference is that   in both photos |

> **Exam tip**
>
> While your partner is talking, think about your own opinion on the topic as the examiner will ask you a question at the end. You only need to say a sentence or two.

56 UNIT 7 SPEAKING

7 WRITING

Part 2: Letter and email

1 Read this exam task and the letter from Anna on the right. Work in pairs to complete the letter with the words and phrases in the box below.

> You have received this letter from your English friend Lauren.
>
> ... and I'm doing a project at school. We have to find which famous people teenagers admire, and why. Can you choose a famous person you admire and write and tell me why you admire them? It'll be interesting to see who you've chosen!
>
> Thanks for helping me, Lauren

as a result	comes across as	
despite	even	even though
famous for being	managed to	
nobody could impress me		
one other quality which		
the man who		

2 Highlight the adjectives Anna used to describe Nelson Mandela's personality in the letter.

3 Which famous person would you write about? Work in pairs and do the following.
   1 Tell your partner who you have chosen and why he or she is or was famous.
   2 Tick (✔) any of the adjectives in the letter you can use to describe him or her.
   3 Make a note of any other adjectives you want to use below.

4 Write your own answer to Lauren.

   Remember to:
   • begin and end your letter correctly.
   • start by saying who you admire and why.
   • explain why the person is or was famous.
   • use some of the linking words and adjectives in Exercises 1 and 2.

Dear Lauren

You asked me to tell you about a famous person I admire. Well, that's easy! (1) .... more than Nelson Mandela!

Mandela was (2) .... the first black president of South Africa, and for being (3) .... brought freedom to his people. (4) .... spending 27 years in prison, he never got discouraged. He (5) .... keep smiling, stay optimistic and be cheerful. He never, ever gave up. He was amazingly confident and (6) .... of this belief in himself he achieved the most amazing things. (7) .... he was fighting a very cruel system, he was always patient, polite and thoughtful to those around him. He was originally a lawyer and (8) .... some of the warders in the prison admired him.

There is (9) .... I really like. If you look at the photos and videos of him, you can see he was always laughing and smiling. There are photos of him dancing and meeting famous singers and film stars when he was president. He loved life and music! He (10) .... such a great guy! I wish I had met him.

I hope you like what I've written.

Best wishes,

Anna

5 Is there a person in your family, or a student in your school/college that you admire? Work in pairs and do the following.
   1 Tell your partner who you have chosen and why.
   2 Write down any adjectives you can use to describe him/her.
   3 Do one of the exam tasks below.

Exam task

Write an answer to one of these exam tasks. Write 140–190 words in an appropriate style.

1 You have received this email from your Australian friend, Andrew.

> I'm doing a project at school. We have to find out which person in their family teenagers admire, and why. Can you choose one person in your family who you admire and write and tell me why?
>
> Thanks for helping me.
>
> Andrew

Write your **email**.

2 You have received this email from your friend, Julia.

> We're doing a project in our English class. We have to find out which student in their school or college other students admire, and why. Can you choose one student you admire and write and tell me why?
>
> Thanks.
>
> Julia

Write your **email**.

Ⓦ *See pages 89–90*

People and feelings

7 READING AND USE OF ENGLISH

Part 5

1 Read the following text. Tick (✔) the adjectives which describe the writer's feelings. You can tick more than one adjective.

amused ☐   annoyed ☐   angry ☐   ashamed ☐   concerned ☐
curious ☐   furious ☐   guilty ☐   irritated ☐   upset ☐

> As Olivia came into the room, she glanced around in that irritating way she sometimes has, trying to decide if it was worth coming into the crowded room. Then she noticed the birthday cake on the table and obviously decided it was. I was standing with my friends and I looked up and half smiled at her, waiting for her to say 'Hi'. Although I had to move out of her way to let her pass, she turned her head and walked right on with her usual confidence, as if she'd never seen me before, and found a space for herself on the sofa. I carried on talking to my friends and stopped myself going over and telling her what I thought of her. That wouldn't have been a good idea while I was so mad at her!

2 Now answer this exam question about the text.

How did the writer feel?
A irritated that Olivia had arrived at the party so late
B angry that he found it less easy to make friends than Olivia
C annoyed that Olivia deliberately took no notice of him
D upset that he didn't have the confidence to speak to Olivia

> **Exam tip ›**
>
> Read the whole of each option carefully and check what the text says. Some of the words in an option may be in the text (e.g. *irritate*, *confidence*) but it doesn't mean that option is the right answer.

3 Read the extract below quickly to get an idea of what it is about. Ask yourself questions while you read: Who? Why? Where? How are people in the text feeling?

4 Work in pairs to discuss your answers.

Exam task

You are going to read an extract from a novel about a girl who has just moved to live in a new place. For questions 1–6, choose the answer (A, B, C or D) which you think fits best according to the text.

> The very first time I saw Andy Byron, I was wandering about in the woods below my new home and thinking about my lonely fate, so when I realised that I wasn't actually alone, I felt cheated. What was this boy doing, cluttering up the picturesque scene? There he stood on the wooden bridge at the foot of the hill, leaning on the rail and completely blocking my way across.
>
> Of course, I didn't have to cross the river. I could go back to the new house in time for Mum's return from the shops, but I wasn't going to let some boy prevent me from exploring my new surroundings. So I hurried down the hill and onto the bridge. He barely looked at me, and moved over just enough for me to get past. I stamped on, my tatty old trainers slapping against the boards, and then swung right, as though I knew where I was going.

In fact, there was a path alongside the river, probably full of joggers and cyclists at weekends, but completely empty on a sunny weekday morning like this one. Nobody for miles around except for me and the boy on the bridge. And anyway, what was he doing here? I had the day off school in order to help Mum with the move, but what was his excuse? Despite myself, I slowed down as the path meandered through a group of what even I recognised as birch trees, and glanced back. And precisely as I did so, he looked up and our eyes met. I was so furious with myself that I turned sharply away, but even before I'd turned, he had dropped his gaze back to the water.

But the incident brought back the bad temper against which I'd been struggling all day. I'd just been telling myself that I didn't really mind moving out here from Edinburgh, and that the spring flowers were actually quite pretty, and the very first person I meet is this hateful boy! I sat down on a big stone and stared gloomily into the river. It was just fate that I'd been dragged away from all my friends and brought here to the end of the bus route. I couldn't even blame Mum and Dad, so I just sat there feeling sorry for myself. Suddenly I caught sight of my watch and jumped to my feet. Midday! Mum would be back now with her load of scrubbing brushes and cleaning products and I hadn't finished washing out the kitchen cupboards.

When I got home, we both worked hard for an hour. Only then did Mum allow us to stop for a coffee. To keep out of her way, I took boxes of stuff upstairs and put them in a corner. One was full of Mum's dancing trophies, which she won't put on display, no matter how much we nag her and keep on at her   line 43
to do so, but the other seemed to contain nothing but rubbish. Why were we carrying all this stuff from one place to another?

I sat down on the floor and began to sort through the junk. Perhaps I could get Mum to get rid of some of it? And then, as I dug into the box, my fingers met something luxuriously soft. Puzzled, I pulled it out and found myself holding a blue velvet drawstring bag with a squarish object inside. I turned it over in my hands, digging my fingernails into the dense, almost furry material. There was a line of embroidery around the top, a row of little suns and moons and stars, decorated with shiny sequins. I told myself sensibly that it wouldn't hold anything exciting, just broken jewellery or dry make-up. But I was rejecting these thoughts even as I lined them up. I just knew that this carefully decorated bag must contain something special.

1 Why did the girl feel cheated?
  A She hadn't realised how lonely she would feel.
  B She didn't want to see anyone else.
  C She found the area less attractive than she had expected.
  D She now felt obliged to go down to the bridge.

2 As the girl crossed the bridge, she wanted to give the impression that she
  A had only just noticed the boy there.
  B had made a sudden decision.
  C wasn't a very friendly person.
  D wouldn't let anything get in her way.

3 The girl was angry with herself in the third paragraph because she
  A was unable to go as fast as she wanted.
  B should have kept looking ahead.
  C was going in the wrong direction.
  D had quickly lost the boy's attention.

4 How does the girl feel in the fourth paragraph after the incident with the boy?
  A disappointed that she had to go back to help her mother
  B upset with her parents for making her move
  C annoyed that it had changed her mood
  D irritated with herself for wasting so much time

5 What does 'nag her' mean in line 43?
  A congratulate her
  B annoy her
  C aim to inform her
  D try to persuade her

6 How does the girl react when she finds the bag?
  A She realises it is different from the other things she has come across.
  B She is certain her expectations of its contents will be disappointed.
  C She is immediately aware she should be careful when she opens it.
  D She thinks it probably isn't as old as it looks and feels.

READING AND USE OF ENGLISH

Part 4

Grammar – Reported speech G *See page 84*

Later in the evening the girl and her mother sat on the sofa together after cleaning the new house.

1 Read the conversation between the girl from the text on pages 58–59 and her mother. Complete the reported speech in the text below.

> How are you? You seem very quiet.

> I'm feeling a bit sad because I've lived in Edinburgh all my life and now I'll have to make new friends. While you were shopping, I went for a walk and I saw a boy on the bridge. I wonder who he is.

> Cheer up. Do you want to come shopping with me tomorrow to buy things we need for the house?

The girl's mum asked her how she (1) .... and said she (2) .... very quiet. The girl said to her that she (3) .... a bit sad because she (4) .... in Edinburgh all her life and now she (5) .... make new friends. She said that while her mum (6) .... shopping, she (7) .... for a walk and she (8) .... a boy on the bridge. She wondered who he (9) .... Her mum told her to (10) .... and asked if she (11) .... to go shopping with her the next day to buy things they (12) .... for the house.

2 Underline the verbs in the speech bubbles and those you have written. Complete this table.

Tense in direct speech	Tense in reported speech
present simple	past simple
present continuous	
present perfect simple	
will	
past continuous	
past simple	

3 Look at these two questions from Exercise 1. Write the reported sentences. When do we use *if* in the reported sentence?

> How are you?

The girl's mum asked her ....

> Do you want to come shopping?

The girl's mum asked ....

4 Now report these questions.

1 Why are you so late?
The teacher asked the boy ....

2 What are you watching?
The girl's father asked her ....

3 Did you score a goal?
The woman asked the boy ....

4 Is there any food left?
The girl asked her mother ....

5 When will you be home?
The boy's mother asked him ....

6 Have you seen my bag?
The boy asked his sister ....

5 Which of these verbs fit into the gap in the sentence below? Which ones don't fit? Why?

> advised   agreed   asked
> encouraged   explained   mentioned
> persuaded   reminded   said   told
> warned

The girl's mum .... her to clean the kitchen.

6 Choose the correct verb in these sentences.

1. The teacher *reminded / explained* the children to bring the money for the trip.
2. We all *agreed / advised* to meet in the park that afternoon.
3. The weather forecaster *told / warned* that it might snow.
4. You didn't *mention / remind* that Fiona was coming too.

7 👁 Exam candidates often make mistakes with reported speech. Choose the correct verb in these sentences.

1. They *told / said* that the weekend would cost £100 but that's not true because it cost only £60 including lunch.
2. Anna *told / said* her friend that there was nothing to be afraid of.
3. In your letter you *told / asked* me if there was anything to see around Lake Frène.
4. Angela *told / said* her cousin not to wait for her.
5. So, the next day Pat went and *told to / told* his sister Mary that her friends were organising a surprise party for her birthday.
6. I *asked / said* my friend to wait for me.
7. Finally, I gave them the address and *told them / told* who I was.
8. When I *asked to / asked* my parents for permission, the answer was clear.

Exam task

For questions 1–6, complete the second sentence so that it has a similar meaning to the first sentence, using the word given. Do not change the word given. You must use between two and five words, including the word given.

Example

I stopped learning to play the drums because the neighbours complained.
GAVE
The neighbours complained about the drums *so I gave up* learning to play them.

1. When I dropped my purse, a kind woman picked it up and ran after me.
BY
When I dropped my purse, ... a kind woman who ran after me.

2. 'Don't leave your wet towel on the floor, Petra,' said her mum.
TOLD
Petra's mum .... leave her wet towel on the floor.

3. The teacher asked if anyone knew the age of the building.
HOW
The teacher said: '............................ old the building is?'

4. The film went on so long that they missed the bus home.
SUCH
It was .... that they missed the bus home.

5. I didn't let my brother borrow my new football yesterday because he lost the last one.
LENT
I .... my brother my new football if he hadn't lost the last one.

6. My aunt said it was better for us to stay away from the old farmhouse.
NOT
My aunt warned .... near the old farmhouse.

Exam tip ›

Never leave an answer blank as each question is worth two marks in Reading and Use of English Part 4.

8 Keeping up to date
READING AND USE OF ENGLISH

Science

3 Which science subject(s) do you like best? Why is it important to study science? Why do you think some people don't like studying science?

Exam task

You are going to read an article about some young scientists who entered a competition. For questions 1–10, choose from the people (A–D). The people may be chosen more than once.

Which person

suggests taking a break and coming back to an idea?	1
recommends asking people to come up with ideas for a project?	2
advises against changing an idea once work has started on it?	3
says presenting information in a variety of ways makes it accessible to more people?	4
advises that a project should be achievable in terms of its aims?	5
says original ideas are likely to be more successful in the competition?	6
suggests a way of researching presentation techniques?	7
says being able to communicate ideas is more valuable than a vast amount of knowledge?	8
mentions that research of the topic should be as extensive as possible?	9
says the amount of effort required to get ready for the competition was challenging?	10

Part 7

1 Which subject are the students studying in each photo? Describe what they are doing.

Here are some of the words you might need to use.

> carry out an experiment/survey   do calculations
> investigate   solve an equation
> substance   test tube

2 Put these topics from a science course in the correct column. Some topics can go in more than one column. Are you studying any of these topics at the moment? Which ones?

> ~~acids~~ ~~algebra~~ ~~atoms~~ ~~the human body~~ cells
> ~~conservation~~ diseases ecosystems electricity
> endangered species fractions gases geometry
> genetics heat light plastics mirrors percentages
> plants pollution recycling sound

ecology	biology	chemistry	physics	mathematics
conservation	the human body	acids	atoms	algebra

62 UNIT 8 READING AND USE OF ENGLISH

> **Exam tip**
>
> Don't choose your answer just because a text mentions something similar to the question, e.g. more than one person talks about ideas (Q1) but only one suggests taking a break.

Young Scientist Award

Four finalists from the Young Scientist Award competition talk about making a video and giving presentations to the judges.

A Maria *investigated the effects of energy drinks and produced one herself.*

Judges look for kids who are really excited about science. You might get inspired by topics which other kids have covered in the past and go on from there. But the judges are really looking for someone who has imagination. If you can make them say, 'Wow, I didn't think of that!', you're off to a good start. If you're having an idea-block, wait a day or two and look at it with fresh eyes. You'll find inspiration somewhere. But make sure that you have enough time to complete your video! Waiting until the last minute, when you are all rushed and stressed, isn't a good idea. If you have a plan laid out before you start anything, it helps keep you on track. Don't submit your video until you've got some feedback. Ask friends whose opinions you can trust to tell you what they really think.

B Erik *invented a substance which can be painted on football boots to stop them attracting mud.*

The other students taking part in the competition, who I got to know really well, came from all over the country. The preparation before the day puts your commitment and determination to the test but it's more than worthwhile! I think the best ideas come from everyday life – because that's where they are going to be put to use after all! Start brainstorming with your family and friends and write down every possibility which comes into your head. But make sure your project is realistic – it's pointless thinking you can stop global warming, for instance, as you don't have that much time or resources.

C David *has found a way of calculating how long bicycle tyres will last.*

I just want to know how everything in the universe works and survives, even though all that information would probably make my brain explode. I knew loads of smart kids would enter, so I didn't think I had a chance at first. For your video, pick a concept that you can explain so that it's visual and interesting. People have different learning styles, so use different approaches to explain the same concept. Be enthusiastic about your topic and your viewers will be enthusiastic, too. There were definitely some finalists who had memorised a lot more science facts than me, but I was able to take a scientific concept and explain it in a simple way – in front of judges, television cameras and an audience. It worked for me!

D Anita *produced lights which come on and go off automatically and can be attached to a bicycle or scooter.*

Entering this competition was a great experience for me. It's easy to feel unsure about your idea, get discouraged and think you should come up with something better, but stick with it. And remember it's best if you know your topic inside out before you even begin to make the video. Making a brilliant video, which gets all the ideas across, isn't as easy as it looks, so it's good to look at past entries from finalists and learn what factors contributed to making them succesful. And one of the hardest parts is fitting your information into two minutes. It seems like plenty of time, but it goes by so quickly! Finally, there's nothing worse than getting everything ready and then finding out that a basic component of the video is wrong. So even if you think it's fine, play it through one last time.

8 WRITING

Part 1: Essay

Grammar – Relative clauses G See page 85

1 Complete these sentences from the texts on page 63 with *who*, *which* or *whose*. Go back to the text if you need to.

Defining clauses
1 But the judges are really looking for someone .... has imagination.
2 Write down every possibility .... comes into your head.
3 You might get inspired by topics .... other kids have covered in the past.
4 Ask friends .... opinions you can trust.

Non-defining clauses
5 Making a brilliant video, ... gets all the ideas across, isn't as easy as it looks.
6 The other students, ... I got to know really well, came from all over the country.

2 Now answer these questions.
1 In which sentence could you omit the relative pronoun? Why?
2 In which sentences could you put *that* instead of *who* or *which*?
3 What is the difference in punctuation between defining and non-defining clauses?

3 Read the question and the first two paragraphs of a candidate's essay. Complete the text with relative pronouns, indicating where *that* or no pronoun are possible alternatives.

All students should study science until they are at least 18. Do you agree?
Notes
Write about:
  1. which jobs need knowledge of science
  2. whether all students are good at science
  3. .... (your own idea)

I certainly agree that all students should study science at school. It's a subject **(1)** .... is incredibly important in our world today. However, I think the issue of how long students should study it is more difficult. If you are the kind of student **(2)** .... main interest is to become a doctor or a physicist, then certainly you will want to study science until you are 18. You will probably enjoy it too, because science is the subject **(3)** .... you are interested in, and probably the

one **(4)** .... you are good at.
But less able students, **(5)** .... find it difficult to pass exams in physics, biology and chemistry, will not be enthusiastic. These subjects, **(6)** .... can be hard at higher levels, may prove too challenging for them. The students will then get very frustrated with science, **(7)** .... means they will behave badly in class. That will make things very difficult for the teachers **(8)** .... are responsible for them.

4 Read these two possible conclusions to the essay. Are they both suitable? Why? / Why not?

A
> Therefore, I would like to conclude by saying that for the reasons I have given above, all students should study science until they are 18. It will be an advantage for every country to have students who are well trained in science.

B
> In my country, students study science until they are 16, and then choose whatever subjects they like until they are 18. I think this is a good system. I would therefore like to conclude by saying that I do not agree that all students should study science until the age of 18.

5 It is important to plan an essay before you start writing. With your partner, complete the plan for the essay in Exercise 3.

Paragraph 1: *good for everyone to study science (important subject) good to study till 18 if …*
Paragraph 2:
Paragraph 3:

6 These phrases can begin or end an essay. Mark them B or E.
1 I would like to conclude by saying that …
2 To start my discussion of this question, I would say that …
3 The first thing I would like to say is …
4 To conclude, I would say that …
5 I will close by saying that I understand both points of view …
6 My first reaction to this question is that …

> **Exam tip**
>
> You can improve the mark for your essay by using a range of vocabulary to express your ideas.

7 Read the question and choose the correct verbs in this essay. Use a dictionary if you need to.

Some people say it is too late to do anything about the problem of global warming. What do you think?

Notes
Write about:
  1. what scientists say about global warming
  2. what problems different countries have
  3. .... (your own idea)

Scientists (**1**) *discovered / identified* some years ago that our planet was getting warmer. They (**2**) *reveal / argue* that humans have caused this problem, because we are using up all our resources like water, and polluting the earth. They (**3**) *claim / conclude* that the atmosphere is now much thinner, and that the sun is now making our planet warmer each year. They have (**4**) *believed / warned* us that there will be major problems as a result of this.

In fact, most scientists would (**5**) *say / report* that the problems are already with us. Some people therefore (**6**) *think / express* that it is too late for us to do anything about it. We have floods, fires, drought in poor countries, terrible pollution in rich countries; there is nothing we can do.

I think governments should (**7**) *encourage / suggest* us all to live in a much greener way. Like many young people, I am optimistic and I (**8**) *disagree / agree* with the idea that it is too late to do anything. But it is really important that politicians all work together. One or two countries on their own can't solve everything.

8 Work in pairs. Discuss these questions.
  1. How many paragraphs are there?
  2. Do you think it is an effective answer to the question?
  3. Are you optimistic or pessimistic about the problems caused by global warming? Why?

9 It's useful to use topic-specific vocabulary in your essay. Make a list of any vocabulary or phrases about global warming in the essay that you could use in one of your own.

Exam task

Write an answer to the essay question below. Write your answer in 140–190 words in an appropriate style, for homework.

In your English class you have been talking about the part robots will play in the future. Now your English teacher has asked you to write an essay for homework:

Write your essay using **all** the notes and giving reasons for your point of view.

Do you think in future it will be possible for robots to become doctors and teachers?

Notes
Write about:
  1. the skills robots have
  2. the feelings of patients and pupils
  3. .... (your own idea)

- Remember your argument must be logical, so plan your essay carefully.
- Make sure you answer the question, use both the prompts, add an idea of your own and come to a clear conclusion.

W *See pages 86–87*

READING AND USE OF ENGLISH

Part 3

Vocabulary – Computers

1 Look at this diagram showing useful computer words. Complete the diagram with these words, then add some more that you use.

browser   email   log out   spreadsheet   update   webcam

```
                install
        icon      (1)
                        application
    (2)                         search – Google – hit
        Software                            secure
                        program     website — bookmark
network  signal
                            Internet        log in   /(3)
     broadband                     browse          password
(4)                 COMPUTER              (5)
attachment  spam   desktop/laptop
                                    chip
       (6)
    microphone
                        screen/monitor
                    hard drive
                bug            data      display
                    backup  crash
```

2 Read these short texts about computers. Complete them with words from the diagram, in the correct form.

> The Neptune is a powerful new laptop. With your purchase, we are offering an external hard (1) .... at a reduced price so you can automatically (2) .... up your files and store large amounts of (3) ....

> You will be logged out of this website if there is no activity for more than ten minutes. Enter your (4) .... and email address to (5) .... in again. Don't forget to (6) .... this site so you can find it again easily.
>
> OK   Cancel

> Software updates are ready to be (7) .... Close any open (8) .... and then restart your computer.
>
> OK   Cancel

Vocabulary – Word building (3)

3 Find words in Exercises 1 and 2 which are formed from the words below plus a suffix.

apply   attach   automatic
easy   power

Now complete the table below with words formed by adding one or two of these prefixes/suffixes.

-d   dis-   -(i)al   en-   -(il)ity   -(it)ion
-(it)ive   -(it)or   -ly   un-

Verb	Noun	Adjective	Adverb
disable	....	ABLE	ably
....	....	....	....
....	COMMERCE	....	....
COMPETE	....	....	....
	....	....	....

4 Which of these suffixes are always added to make nouns and which to make adjectives?

-d   -al   -ity   -tion   -ive   -or

To make nouns, add: ....
To make adjectives, add: ....

> **Exam tip**
>
> In Reading and Use of English Part 3 there is always one word which has to be changed by adding a prefix (and sometimes a suffix too!).

5 Read this text to get a general understanding of what it is about. Some words are missing. For each gap decide if you need a noun, adjective or adverb.

Laptop computers

Portable computers first became (1) .... available in 1981 but they were large and heavy, about the size of a microwave! Although they marked the beginning of (2) .... advances in the computer industry, they lacked the (3) .... to work on a battery, so they never really gained in (4) .... Fortunately, work continued to reduce their (5) .... and size but it took another ten years of (6) .... in the computer industry before people started to buy them in large numbers. The older models were (7) .... too heavy and big to be on your lap but the name laptop became widely used. The laptop of today is (8) .... next to those earlier models but is now in (9) .... with smartphones and tablets, which have become very (10) .... and do almost anything you might want!

---

6 Now use one or two of the prefixes/suffixes to change the words below so that they fit the gaps in the text in Exercise 5. (You do not need to use all the prefixes/suffixes.)

| -able | -d | dis- | -ful | -al | -ly | -ity |
| -ion | -ive | -or | -ment | -t | un- | |

1 commerce — commercially
2 technology — ....
3 able — ....
4 popular — ....
5 weigh — ....
6 develop — ....
7 actual — ....
8 recognise — ....
9 compete — ....
10 power — ....

7 Look back at the words in the gaps. Which one of them contains a prefix? Can you make any of the others negative by adding the prefix *un-* or *in-*?

8 Now make these words negative. Use one of the prefixes *dis-*, *im-*, *il-*, *in-*, *ir-*, *mis-* or *un-*.

approval   experienced   fortunate   honesty   legal   patient
polite   reliable   responsible   satisfied   understanding

Exam task

For questions 1–8, read the text below. Use the word given in capitals at the end of some of the lines to form a word that fits in the gap in the same line. There is an example at the beginning (0).

> **Exam tip**
>
> Read the text through before you begin, and read it again when you have finished, to be sure it makes sense with the new words you have written.

A SAILING BIKE

A teenager called Ned Aufenast has come up with an (0) *impressive* way of getting about. It is a bicycle with a sail and it's quite a (1) .... sight as Ned rides it through the traffic near his home. (2) .... he wasn't sure if he could ride it on the road but, once he had given it independent brakes, lights and reflectors, he was given (3) .... to ride it anywhere except on motorways, where he would be doing so (4) ....

Ned says he was inspired one day when he was riding his bicycle. It was a real struggle because of the (5) .... of the wind. He's always been (6) .... about sailing and thought it might be fun to use wind power on the road. He says: 'You just pedal and the wind helps you to go faster.' Although not essential, his (7) .... of sailing was very (8) .... when he was designing the bike.

IMPRESS
DRAMA

INITIAL

PERMIT

LEGAL

STRONG
PASSION

KNOW
HELP

67

8 SPEAKING

Part 3

1 Work in pairs. Talk about the two things in the pictures. Give reasons for your answers.

How often do you use them?
How important are they to you?
Who in your family are they most important to?

2 **22** Listen to two students discussing this question:

> How important are these inventions in our daily lives?
> fridge   TV   car   bicycle   laptop

1 Do they take turns to talk?
2 Do they ask each other's opinions?
3 Do they always agree?
4 Do they talk about each picture?

3 **22** Listen again. Write down what they say:

1 to start the conversation.
2 when they move to the next item.
3 to ask each other's opinions.
4 when they agree with each other.

4 How many words/phrases can you think of that mean the same as *important*? Write them down.

5 **22** It is better not to use the same word too many times. Listen again and add the words/phrases they use for *important* to your list. Did you already have some of them on your list?

6 **23** Now listen to the students discussing the second part of the test.

> Which two do you think will become less important in the future?

What do they decide? Does it matter if they don't agree?

7 **23** Listen again. Write down what they say.

1 How does Karolina begin?
2 What does Miguel say when he asks Karolina's opinion?
3 What does Miguel say about the bicycle to show he hasn't changed his mind?

Exam task

Work in pairs. Time your discussion. If it is too short, think of other things you can say.

Here are some inventions that many people think are important in our daily lives.

Talk to each other about how important these things are in our daily lives.

- washing machine
- phone
- laptop
- TV
- microwave

How important are these inventions in our daily lives?

Now you have a minute to decide which two you think will become more important in the future.

> **Exam tip**
>
> Don't spend too long discussing one item. You only have three minutes for the whole conversation. Learn phrases you can use to move the conversation forwards. See Units 4 and 6.

Part 4

Exam task

Discuss these questions with a partner.

- How important is technology at school? Which subjects is it essential for? Why?
- Do you enjoy watching TV? What programmes do you like? Why?
- Do you think the use of technology has stopped people from talking to each other? Why / Why not?
- Do you think people are too dependent on mobile phones? Why / Why not?
- Some people say young children shouldn't watch TV. Do you agree? Why / Why not?

> **Exam tip**
>
> When you answer a question, think about why, when or how. Always extend your answer.

8 LISTENING

Part 1

> **Exam tip**
>
> When you first see the question and possible answers, try to identify what the situation is and what you are being asked to do. It will help you to choose the correct answer.

1 Work in pairs. Quickly read the eight questions below and match the situations with A–H.

A explaining an intention .....
B expressing feelings about what happened .....
C identifying a problem .....
D identifying travel details .....
E describing the weather for an event .....
F giving an opinion about something .....
G suggesting an activity others would like .....
H giving a purpose for speaking .....

Exam task

24 You will hear people talking in eight different situations. For questions 1–8, choose the best answer, A, B or C.

1 You hear a brother and sister talking.
   What happened to the boy's work?
   A He lost it when the laptop crashed.
   B He saved it in the wrong place.
   C He forgot to save it.

2 You hear a sports programme on the radio.
   Conditions for the race will be
   A clear and sunny.
   B wet and muddy.
   C cold and icy.

3 You hear a teacher talking to his class.
   Why is he talking to them?
   A to make a request
   B to pass on a complaint
   C to give instructions

4 You hear a boy and girl talking about school.
   What does the girl think of her maths lessons?
   A They're not well taught.
   B They're not very challenging.
   C They're not practical enough for her.

5 You hear a boy talking to his sister about a shopping trip.
   What does the boy say about the shopping trip?
   A He regretted playing a trick on his friends.
   B He was worried about losing his friends.
   C He and his friends disliked the crowds.

6 You hear a girl talking to her class about her visit to an aquarium.
   What part of the visit does she recommend?
   A walking through the glass tunnels
   B handling some very unusual fish
   C seeing a marine art exhibition

7 You hear a boy talking about a cookery competition he entered.
   What is he aiming to do?
   A complain about what went wrong with a recipe
   B give instructions on how to make a difficult recipe
   C explain why he chose a particular recipe

8 You hear a father and daughter talking about a holiday.
   The family will get to the holiday centre
   A by train.
   B by car.
   C by coach.

LISTENING UNIT 8 69

REVISION

Units 1 and 2

1 Choose the correct answer.

1. Don't forget to text me when you *arrive / 'll arrive*.
2. This is a great place to stay. We *camp / 're camping* in a farmer's field.
3. Sorry, I *'m not understanding / don't understand* what you're saying.
4. This time next week we *'ll sit / 'll be sitting* on the beach in the sun.
5. Paul says he knows that man but I *don't recognise / 'm not recognising* him.
6. I'll ring you back – I can't talk to you now because I *do / 'm doing* my homework.
7. Let me know as soon as you *hear / 'll hear* from Kamilla.
8. Children who *come / are coming* from large families get used to sharing their things.

2 Complete the second sentence so that it has a similar meaning to the first sentence, using the word given. Do not change the word given. You must use between two and five words, including the word given.

1. Usually, a modern city has wider streets than a historic city.
   AS
   Usually, the streets in a historic city .... those in a modern city.

2. Industrial areas tend to be very noisy compared to rural areas.
   FAR
   There is usually .... in industrial areas than in rural areas.

3. It takes my brother two hours to get to work but our father has a two-minute walk.
   MUCH
   My brother's journey to work .... our father's.

4. My favourite café is near the market square.
   BEST
   The café which I .... from the market square.

5. My friends and I don't go to the cinema as often as our parents do.
   LESS
   My friends and I go to the cinema .... our parents do.

3 Decide which word (A, B, C or D) best fits each gap.

1. There was a .... of opinion in my family about where to go on holiday, so in the end we stayed at home.
   A variation   B contrast   C difference   D disagreement

2. We found a quiet .... to have a picnic.
   A point   B spot   C situation   D site

3. My dad is going to make a .... decision tonight about whether I can go on the trip.
   A last   B latest   C finishing   D final

4. If you go on a cycle ride, you will get lots of .... air.
   A fresh   B pure   C clean   D natural

5. Peter wears strange clothes to .... attention to himself.
   A pull   B draw   C focus   D catch

6. If you want to be good at basketball, you will need to .... an effort to practise.
   A do   B give   C make   D take

7. When Fiona realised her secret had been discovered, she knew she was in serious ....
   A trouble   B problem   C fault   D concern

8. I practised .... my breath for ages so I could swim underwater.
   A keeping   B cutting   C stopping   D holding

4 Read this email and correct the mistakes in the underlined verbs.

Hi Dave
Thanks for letting me know that you and your family (1) <u>are being</u> there to meet me next Friday when (2) <u>I'll arrive</u> at the airport. My flight from Milan (3) <u>is going to arrive</u> at 16.00. (4) <u>I'm thinking</u> that (5) <u>it will be taking</u> about 45 minutes to go through passport control, collect my luggage and pass through customs, so as soon as (6) <u>I'll have done</u> that (7) <u>I'll be coming</u> and find you in the arrivals hall.

(8) <u>I'll be looking forward</u> to getting to know your parents. You've told me so much about them, I feel (9) <u>I'm knowing</u> them already!

You asked me what I would like to do while (10) <u>I stay</u> with you. That's easy – I would like to meet some of your friends and to go to some of the places that you and your family (11) <u>are liking</u>. And I'd like to visit a castle, if you think there (12) <u>'s going to be</u> time, because (13) <u>I'll have never seen</u> one before. (14) <u>Will there be</u> one anywhere near where (15) <u>you're living</u>?

See you soon,
Giorgio

5 Match the two halves of the sentences and put the verbs into the correct past tense.

1 I hurt my hand
2 We got to the party so late that
3 We've been best friends
4 I've been trying to download this game for hours
5 I rang your doorbell six times yesterday
6 I've been to the new leisure park several times
7 I was playing the computer game you gave me
8 When I first met you last year,

a but you ……………… (not answer) so I went away.
b but I ……………… (not manage) to do it yet.
c when you ……………… (phone) me.
d while I ……………… (play) tennis.
e I was sure I ……………… (see) you before somewhere.
f our friends ……………… (already go) home.
g but I ……………… (not eat) in the café there yet.
h since you ……………… (come) to this school.

6 Complete the text with the verbs from the box, in the correct tense.

> be be go have invite
> know let sail set shine

My brother (1) ……………… sailing every weekend with his friends. He always says, 'When you (2) ……………… a bit older you can come with me.' I (3) ……………… fourteen next summer, so maybe he (4) ……………… me go with him then. My uncle loves sailing and has a boat too. Last weekend he (5) ……………… me to go out with him. I (6) ……………… (never) with him before so I was really pleased. When we (7) ……………… out, the sun (8) ……………… but after about half an hour it got very windy. I (9) ……………… sailing lessons since September, so I (10) ……………… exactly what to do. My brother was really surprised when we got back and my uncle told him what a great sailor I am!

7 Complete the sentences with adverbs formed from the adjectives in the box. Use each adjective only once.

> careful definite easy excited immediate
> particular simple usual

1 The children ran round and round ……………… while they waited for the show to begin.
2 Michael says he's ……………… coming with us to the pool tomorrow.
3 Jonnie has a real talent for languages – he learns them ……………… .
4 Football practice was due to start in ten minutes so we had to get changed ……………… .
5 I ……………… listen to music in bed while I'm going to sleep.
6 I carried the birthday cake to the table very ……………… as I didn't want to drop it!
7 I explained as ……………… as I could but they still didn't understand.
8 Emma was ……………… good at maths so the school entered her in a competition.

8 Complete the sentences with an adjective formed from one of the words in the box.

> adventure centre fury mystery nature
> predict rely suit

1 There was a knock at the door, but nobody was there when we opened it – it was very ……………… .
2 This film isn't ……………… for my little sister as she's only six.
3 My parents like to go to the same place on holiday – they're not very ……………… .
4 Our neighbour is looking for someone ……………… to babysit who will come every week at the same time.
5 It's ……………… to feel a bit worried when you do something for the first time.
6 My brother was ……………… when he realised I'd worn his jeans.
7 Dad always makes the same jokes when my friends come round – he's so ……………… .
8 My school is very ……………… , so it's near all the shops.

REVISION 71

Units 3 and 4

1 Choose the correct linking words.

1 *Despite / While* she was an excellent singer, Joanna could not play any musical instruments.
2 *Although / However* I have always liked travelling, I really dislike flying.
3 *Even though / In spite of* he is very good at maths, Peter simply isn't interested in it.
4 *Although / While* Paul tried hard to get to the concert on time, he arrived late.
5 *However / In spite of* being a great fan of James Bond films, George did not enjoy the latest one.
6 *Even though / However* my little sister likes school, she's always happy when the weekend comes.
7 *However / Despite* enjoying drawing, I wouldn't want to take art classes.
8 *Although / In spite of* I dislike dogs, they've never frightened me.

2 Complete the sentences with a passive verb.

1 Our French teacher cancelled the test because a lot of students were absent.
   Our French test .... because a lot of students were absent.
2 My parents are sending me to a secondary school nearby because they like it.
   I .... to a secondary school nearby because my parents like it.
3 Everyone in my family has played the same piano.
   The same piano .... everyone in my family.
4 My teacher had advised me not to choose anything too ambitious for my science project.
   I .... not to choose anything too ambitious for my science project.
5 The chef will take the biscuits out of the oven in 20 minutes if they're ready.
   The biscuits .... out of the oven in 20 minutes if they're ready.
6 My grandmother is making me a prom dress.
   My prom dress .... by my grandmother.
7 I borrowed those books from the school library.
   Those books .... from the school library.
8 The school is putting the silver cup I won in the 100 metres on a special shelf.
   The silver cup I won in the 100 metres .... on a special shelf at my school.

3 Complete the sentences with a person who works in the film industry.

1 The s........................ t........................ usually checks the quality of the recording on a film.
2 A s........................ normally performs action shots, so the star can avoid dangerous situations.
3 A m........................ a........................ always does an actor's face and hair before he or she goes on set.
4 A p........................ is responsible for raising money to make a film.
5 A c........................ films the scenes and goes on location if necessary.
6 The d........................ guides and instructs the actors on how to perform a scene.
7 A c........................ d........................ creates the clothes the actors wear on set.
8 The s........................ d........................ arranges the scenery on the film set.

4 Which type of film would usually feature the following?

1 a spaceship, time travel and lots of special effects
2 funny scenes that make you laugh
3 a complicated plot with twists and turns
4 interesting factual information
5 cowboys and horses
6 characters that are drawn
7 moving figures or animals rather than real people
8 really frightening scenes, ghosts and monsters
9 car chases and people running across roofs
10 an amusing love story

5 Answer these questions about music.

1 Can you name three musical instruments that have strings?
2 Can you name three wind instruments?
3 Can you name five different types of music?
4 A pop group can also be called a ....
5 The words of a song are called ....
6 The music of a song is called the ....
7 A recording with a number of tracks is called an ....
8 The people who really like a particular band are called ....

6 Choose the correct modal verb (A, B or C) to complete the sentences.

1 You .... always check your homework before you hand it in.
   A ought   B should   C have to
2 You .... go to the party if you promise to be home by 11.00.
   A can   B must   C should
3 You .... to complete all the work for your science projects by next Friday.
   A must   B will have   C can
4 You .... drink any of that milk – it's gone off.
   A don't have to   B needn't   C mustn't
5 You .... won the competition if you hadn't fallen over on the ice!
   A should have   B could have   C must have
6 You .... been training really hard to have done so well in the 100 metres.
   A must have   B ought to have   C could have
7 I .... leave the house at 5.30 a.m. yesterday because the school trip started at 6.00 a.m.
   A could   B should   C had to
8 You .... asked me what to do if you were unsure.
   A needn't have   B should have   C must have

7 Complete these sentences with a preposition in each gap.

1 My brother is much more successful than me, but I've never been jealous .... him at all.
2 When you go on a school trip, your teachers are responsible .... your safety.
3 When the school week starts, I like to talk .... my friends about what I did at the weekend.
4 I've always been interested .... painting, and I'd like to take some art lessons.
5 I don't know if I can spend a week in London; it depends .... the cost of the accommodation.
6 Some elderly people find things to complain .... all the time, but my grandmother never does.
7 Could you possibly help .... the end-of-term party?
8 I'm really excited .... going to the big international hockey match next week.
9 Everyone knows that cold winters with a lot of snow are typical .... Canada!
10 Will you think .... which foreign language you want to study next?

8 Complete each paragraph below with words from the box above it. Add s or 's if necessary. There is one extra word in each list.

defender   goalkeeper   penalty   pitch   referee   tackle

A football match is always played on a (1) .... with a (2) .... making sure the players on both teams play fairly. On each team, it's the attackers' role to score goals and the (3) .... job to keep them out of the goal, with help from two or three (4) .... All the players try to (5) .... the opposition in order to get the ball.

court   net   opponent   point   serve   umpire

In a tennis match it is the (6) .... who keeps the score. The player who starts the match has to (7) .... the ball to his/her (8) .... Every time a (9) .... is played, the ball must go over the (10) ....

9 Complete the lists with the correct form of each word.

	adjective	noun
1	convenient	....
2	equal	....
3	....	generosity
4	independent	....
5	....	patience

	verb	noun
6	conclude	....
7	connect	....
8	....	division
9	expand	....
10	....	persuasion

REVISION 73

Units 5 and 6

1 Match the two halves of the conditional sentences and put the verbs into the correct tense.

1. I might have enjoyed the school concert more
2. If I hadn't learnt to play the guitar,
3. Unless you live a long way away,
4. Take some money with you
5. I'll help you with your project
6. She will be late for school again
7. Most children never get to see a giraffe
8. If I could change one thing about my school,
9. Peter said he would try to learn some Chinese
10. You'll feel terrible in the morning

a. if they .... (start) teaching it at his school.
b. as long as you .... (help) me with mine!
c. unless they .... (go) to a zoo.
d. it .... (be) the uniform.
e. it .... (be) usually best to cycle to school.
f. if you .... (not get) a good night's sleep.
g. I .... (miss) doing something I'm good at.
h. unless she .... (set) her alarm clock.
i. if there .... (be) some singing in it.
j. in case you .... (need) to buy some lunch.

2 Complete the text with the correct form of the words in brackets.

Education in Britain

In Britain, children move to a (1) .... (SECOND) school at the age of 11. The vast (2) .... (MAJOR) of students go to a state school rather than a private one. There is no (3) .... (EXAMINE) you have to pass to get in, and this type of mixed ability school is known as a (4) .... (COMPREHEND) school. However, students are divided into different groups according to their (5) .... (ABLE), a system known as streaming. The most able students go into the top set, where the most (6) .... (CHALLENGE) work is done. All the students study a (7) .... (VARY) of subjects, including English, maths and science, and also have the (8) .... (POSSIBLE) of doing sport, art and music as part of their timetable. At the age of 16, students have the (9) .... (CHOOSE) of which subjects to continue for the next two years, and at 18, those who want to go on to university put in their (10) .... (APPLY).

3 Complete the text with *a*, *an* or *the*, or leave a gap if necessary.

The Climate of Cape Town, South Africa

Cape Town has (1) .... Mediterranean climate, with (2) .... mild, wet winters, and (3) .... dry and very warm summers. In winter, which lasts from (4) .... beginning of June to (5) .... end of August, (6) .... cold weather comes across from (7) .... Atlantic Ocean bringing (8) .... heavy rain and strong winds. (9) .... winter months are cool, with (10) .... minimum temperature of 7 °C (45 °F). Most of (11) .... city's annual rainfall occurs in wintertime, but rainfall amounts for (12) .... different suburbs can vary dramatically. Summer, which lasts from (13) .... November to March, is warm and dry. Cape Town gets frequent strong winds from (14) .... south-east, known locally as the *Cape Doctor*, because they blow away (15) .... pollution and clean (16) .... air in the city. However, Cape Town can be uncomfortably hot when the *berg wind* blows for (17) .... couple of weeks in February or early March. (18) .... Cape Town's weather is in fact remarkably similar to that of San Francisco in (19) .... USA, although it is definitely warmer, with (20) .... average air temperature of 19 °C (66 °F) versus San Francisco's 13 °C (55 °F).

REVISION

4 **Correct the mistakes in these sentences written by exam candidates.**

1 I've never seen so beautiful roses in a garden.
2 When the concert started, everything was such exciting that the time flew.
3 I have so good memories from there, and I'd like to share them with you.
4 The book was such a good that I couldn't put it down.
5 It was great to hold the party on such marvellous evening.
6 I've never eaten a such tasty risotto before.
7 I love clothes and fashion is such important to me.
8 We had so a good laugh last time we met.
9 I have never stayed in a hotel which was such beautiful like this.
10 I had never trained with a such perfect volleyball team before.

5 **Complete these short expressions by writing a word from the box below.**

1 air ....
2 electrical ....
3 email ....
4 fresh ....
5 local ....
6 plastic ....
7 ready ....
8 recycled ....
9 reduce ....
10 take ....

> attachment bags conditioning
> equipment ingredients meals paper
> produce a shower waste

6 **Now complete this text with the expressions from Exercise 5.**

If you want to live in an environmentally friendly way, there are lots of simple, practical steps you can take in your everyday life.
First of all, get your family to understand that it's important to (1) .... at home by cutting your energy consumption whenever possible. For instance, you can (2) .... rather than a bath and always ensure that you turn off (3) .... when you have finished with it. Never leave the television or computer on standby! And if you use the computer a lot, use (4) .... for printing and if at all possible send your homework by (5) .... instead of using paper. In addition, you should try to keep use of (6) .... in the home and family car to a minimum, even when it's very hot.
Remember too that you don't need (7) .... to take your shopping home when you go to the supermarket; it's much better to take a basket or box with you. When you're shopping for food, look for (8) .... rather than food that has been transported from miles away. Finally, if your family commits to healthy eating and you always prepare meals with (9) .... , you can avoid the huge amounts of packaging used to wrap the (10) .... you can find on the chilled counter.

7 **Make adjectives from the words below, then complete the sentences with them.**

competition ....
cheer ....
communicate ....
create ....
decide ....
determine ....
energy ....
sympathy ....

1 When I came home feeling unwell, my mum was very .... towards me.
2 My sister hates to lose – she's so ....
3 I knew I had to be .... , so I chose the answer very rapidly.
4 My grandfather has never been very .... but last week he sent me a long letter.
5 My cousin is very .... and she has just started her own business designing jewellery.
6 I was absolutely .... to pass the exam, so I studied really hard.
7 My best friend is always .... and I've never once seen her in a bad mood.
8 My little brother is incredibly .... and runs about all day without getting tired.

8 **Complete the sentences with the verbs in the box. Use each verb only once.**

> can't imagine dislike have never been able
> is looking forward suggested would like
> would prefer would rather

1 I .... cycle to school than catch the bus every morning.
2 Susie .... to studying another language next year.
3 I .... to go to university if I get good grades in my exams.
4 Alison .... living apart from her twin sister.
5 Tim .... to take up judo rather than play tennis.
6 Most students of my age .... having homework to do every night.
7 I .... to do maths without a calculator.
8 I .... leaving at about 6.00 so we could get to the concert on time.

REVISION 75

Units 7 and 8

1 **Choose the correct answer in italics.**

My family arranged (1) *to go / going* away at the weekend to my uncle's cottage in the mountains. It wasn't a long journey but I still managed (2) *to fall / falling* asleep on the way because it was so hot. My father had hoped (3) *to do / doing* the whole journey without stopping, but we took a break by a lake halfway up the mountain to cool down. Luckily, I had suggested (4) *to take / taking* our swimming things in case we felt like (5) *to swim / swimming* in the stream near the cottage. We enjoyed (6) *to relax / relaxing* by the water for an hour or two and then we carried on (7) *to drive / driving* up the mountain. When we arrived at the cottage, my mother tried (8) *to find / finding* the key in her handbag but it wasn't there. She said she remembered (9) *to put / putting* it in, and she made us (10) *to go / go* through all the other bags. In the end, we had to give up (11) *to look / looking* because it was getting dark. We had to choose between sleeping on the grass or going home, so we decided (12) *to go / going* home. At least we had a nice swim in the lake!

2 **Complete the second sentence so that it has a similar meaning to the first sentence, using the word given. Do not change the word given. You must use between two and five words, including the word given.**

1 James said, 'I can't play football because I'm looking after my brother.'
   EXPLAINED
   James .... play football because he was looking after his brother.

2 Alice said, 'OK, I'll help you with your maths homework.'
   AGREED
   Alice .... me with my maths homework.

3 My friend said he couldn't come with us to the cinema because he'd forgotten his money.
   SO
   My friend said, 'I've forgotten my money, ... with you to the cinema.'

4 My uncle said, 'This is the best show I've seen for years.'
   SUCH
   My uncle said he .... good show for years.

5 Anna said, 'I like your new dress.'
   TOLD
   Anna .... my new dress.

6 Archie asked me, 'Do you know how to play chess?'
   IF
   Archie asked me .... how to play chess.

3 **Complete the sentences with these verbs.**

come dress get get go have
keep look make show suit try

1 I .... in the same way as my friends.
2 I know what styles .... me.
3 I look for clothes that .... me look different from other people.
4 I .... rid of my old clothes when I'm tired of them.
5 Dark colours really don't .... good on me.
6 I like to .... up with the latest fashions.
7 Some people like to .... off by wearing all the latest fashions.
8 As soon as clothes .... out of fashion, I stop wearing them.
9 Sometimes clothes .... back into fashion after a few years.
10 I like to .... things on before I buy them.
11 I .... different tastes from my friends.
12 My friends like to .... dressed up when they go out.

4 **Complete the sentences with these adjectives.**

curious frustrated guilty
optimistic passionate patient

1 Mario has always been .... about basketball and hopes to be a professional player.
2 I was .... because I was trying to buy a ticket for the festival and my laptop wouldn't work.
3 Karim was really good at photography, so he was .... about winning the competition.
4 I was .... to know where Jack was going, so I followed him.
5 Elena felt .... about not going out with her friends as she had promised, so she phoned them all up to apologise.
6 There was a really long queue but we just had to be .... and wait for our turn.

5 These adjectives also fit in some of the gaps in Exercise 4. Which ones? Look at the grammar as well as the meaning.

ashamed .... confident ....
enthusiastic .... furious ....
interested .... irritated ....

6 Complete the text with *who*, *which*, *whose* or *where*. When you have finished, go back and add *that* or – (nothing) to those gaps where they are possible.

Edwin Hubble, (1) .... was born in 1889, was an American astronomer (2) .... work has made a huge contribution to what we know about the universe. There is a telescope, an asteroid and a moon crater (3) .... are all named after him. As a child, Hubble was someone (4) .... was both a bright student and an excellent athlete. He went to the University of Chicago, (5) .... he studied mathematics, astronomy and philosophy. He spent most of his working life in California, (6) .... he formulated Hubble's Law, (7) .... helped astronomers determine the age of the universe and prove that it was expanding. At the time, astronomers knew only about the Milky Way, a galaxy of stars and planets (8) .... the Earth is part of. But with Hubble's work it became clear that there were many more galaxies beyond the Milky Way.

7 Read these definitions, then complete the words they define with the correct consonants.

1. when paper, glass, etc. is put through a process so that it can be used again
   _ E _ _ _ _ I _ _

2. an illness often caused by an infection
   _ I _ E A _ E

3. adjective describing animals and plants which may soon disappear from the world because there are so few left
   E _ _ A _ _ E _ E _

4. the smallest basic unit of a plant or animal
   _ E _ _

5. the protection of nature
   _ O _ _ E _ _ A _ I O _

6. the scientific study of genes which control the particular characteristics of a living thing
   _ E _ E _ I _ _

7. the smallest unit that an element can be divided into
   A _ O _

8. a type of energy that can produce light and heat and make machines work
   E _ E _ _ _ I _ I _ _

8 Complete the sentences with the correct form of the word in capitals at the end of each sentence.

1. You need a lot of .... in your arms to row a boat very far. **STRONG**
2. The argument against smoking is a very .... one. **POWER**
3. Our school was .... much smaller than it is now. **ORIGINAL**
4. We couldn't decide what to do as there were so many .... to choose from. **POSSIBLE**
5. It's .... to leave the table before everyone's finished eating. **POLITE**
6. Not enough young people attend the town festival – we need to make it more .... to them. **ATTRACT**
7. There are too many .... on this channel – they break up the programmes. **COMMERCE**
8. I was told to go to the school at 8.00 a.m. for a meeting but there must have been a .... because nobody was there. **UNDERSTAND**

REVISION 77

GRAMMAR REFERENCE G

Unit 1

Present tenses

We use the present simple
1 to say when things happen if they take place regularly:
   I **meet** my friends on Saturdays.
2 to talk about permanent situations:
   I **live** in a small flat.
3 to state general truths:
   Teenagers **sleep** more than adults.

We use the present continuous
1 to talk about the present moment:
   Go away – I**'m watching** TV.
2 for a temporary action or event:
   I**'m staying** with my granny for a couple of days.
3 for repeated actions and events over a period of time:
   I**'m learning** to play the guitar. (but not exactly at the present moment)
4 for changing or developing situations:
   The world **is getting** warmer.

State verbs

These are generally used in a simple tense (i.e. not a continuous tense). They are mostly about thoughts, feelings, belonging and the senses. Here are some common examples: believe, know, mean, remember, suppose, understand, feel (=believe), think (= believe), adore, despise, hate, like, love, want, wish, prefer, belong, have/have got (= possess), own, smell, taste, hear, see, feel, contain, seem, look (= seem), weigh :
   I **like** our new flat.
   I **have** three sisters.

Present tenses in future clauses

In clauses referring to future time and which begin with when, until, before, after, as soon as, we use the present simple:
   I'll call you when I **get** to my friend's. (not ...when I will get)
or the present perfect:
   I'll have dinner when I**'ve finished** my homework. (not ...when I will have finished)

The future

We use the present simple for scheduled events with a future meaning:
   The bus **leaves** for London at 8.15 on Saturday.
We use the present continuous for plans which are already arranged:
   We're **playing** football on Wednesday.
We use will
1 for decisions made at the moment of speaking:
   The phone's ringing. I**'ll** answer it.
2 for anything which is uncertain, especially with probably, maybe, I think, I hope and I expect:
   I probably **won't finish** this project today.
3 for predictions (as they are not definite):
   The number of people on the planet **will grow** to nine billion by 2050.
4 for requests, promises, offers:
   I**'ll give** you your book back on Friday.

We use going to
1 for something we have decided to do but which isn't a definite arrangement:
   I**'m going to ring** my friend in a minute.
2 to predict something when we have some evidence:
   It**'s going to rain**. (I can see the clouds.)
We can often use either the present continuous or going to for plans:
   I**'m meeting** / I**'m going to meet** my friends in town.
We use the future continuous for an event happening at a particular time or over a period of time in the future:
   I can't come at 6.00 as I**'ll be looking** after my sister.

Comparisons

1 syllable (warm)	2 syllables ending in -y (happy)	2 or more syllables (expensive)
warmer (than)	happier (than)	more expensive (than)
(the) warmest	(the) happiest	the most expensive

Some two-syllable adjectives (e.g. quiet, polite) and adjectives ending in -ow, -er and -le can take both forms:
   Jo is **more polite** than Sam. = Jo is **politer** than Sam.
Irregular adjectives:
   good, better, best
   bad, worse, worst
   far, farther/further, farthest/furthest

We use comparative structures to compare people or things:
1 with an adjective:
   My brother is **taller than** my sister.
   My sister **isn't as tall as** my brother.
   I'm **as good** at football **as** my older brother.
   This TV programme is **less interesting than** last week's.
2 with a noun:
   I get **more/less pocket money** than you.

Unit 2

Past tenses

We use the past simple for:
1. completed actions and events in the past:
   *I **went** to the city centre yesterday.*
2. repeated actions and events in the past:
   *I **practised** the guitar every day before the concert.* (But the concert's over now so I don't practise every day.)
3. permanent or long-term situations in the past:
   *My family **lived** in Paris for four years.* (But they don't now.)

We use the present perfect simple:
1. to talk about a period of time which is still continuing, sometimes with *since* or *for*:
   *I**'ve lived** in this village for five years.* (And I continue to live here.)
2. for unfinished actions and events, sometimes with *still* or *yet*:
   *I **haven't been** to the new pool yet.* (But I hope I will go there.)
3. for events that happened in the recent past, sometimes with *just*:
   *She**'s gone** to the cinema.* (And she's still there.)
4. to talk about how many times something has happened, sometimes with *already*:
   *I**'ve (already) heard** this band several times.*

We use the present perfect continuous (often with *since* or *for*) when we want to emphasise the activity rather than the result.
Compare:
*I**'ve been reading** this book for weeks.* (I still haven't finished it.)
*I**'ve read** four books this week.* (I've finished them.)

*I**'ve been doing** my homework while you've been out.* (That's how I spent the time.)

*I**'ve done** my homework while you've been out.* (I've finished it.)

We use the past continuous:
1. to talk about a particular moment in the past:
   *I **was listening** to the radio at 8.30 this morning.*
2. for an activity beginning before a past action (usually in the past simple) and continuing until or after it:
   *I **was going** upstairs when I **heard** a strange noise.*
3. for two things happening at the same time:
   *It **was pouring** with rain while **we were** playing football.*

We use the past perfect simple:
1. to refer to an earlier time when we are already talking about the past, often with time expressions like *when, after, by the time, as soon as*:
   *By the time I was six, I**'d lived** in three different places.*
2. with adverbs like *just, already, before, ever* and *never*:
   *Jasmine offered to lend me her book but I**'d** already **finished** my homework.*

We use *used to* and *would* to talk about past habits when we are emphasising they are no longer true. *Used to* is more common than *would*:
*My mum **used to sing** to me every night.*
= *My mum **would sing** to me every night.*
Used to can describe actions and states, but *would* can only describe actions:
My brother used to live in Sydney. **not** *My brother would live…*

Adverb formation

Many adverbs are formed from adjectives by adding the suffix *-ly*, but note the following:

Adjectives ending in *-y* change their last letter to *-i* before adding *-ly*: *angry* → *angrily*

Adjectives ending in consonant + *-le* lose the last letter before adding *-ly*: *probable* → *probably*

Adjectives ending in *-e* keep the *-e* and add *-ly*: *rare* → *rarely*

Adjectives ending in *-l* add *-ly*: *careful* → *carefully*

Unit 3

The passive

Active	Passive
Kai **plays** lead guitar.	Lead guitar **is played** by Kai.
The DJ **is playing** my favourite song now.	My favourite song **is being played** by the DJ now.
The band first **recorded** this song in 2009.	This song **was** first **recorded** by the band in 2009.
Lots of people **have sung** this song.	This song **has been sung** by lots of different people.
You **can download** the track for free.	The track **can be downloaded** for free.
The band's fans **will buy** their new album.	The new album **will be bought** by the band's fans.
The shops **had sold** a million copies of the album by midday.	A million copies of the album **had been sold** by midday.

The passive is used when
1. we don't know who or what does/did something:
   My bike **was stolen** from outside the school.
2. the action is more important than who does/did it:
   The match **has been cancelled** because of the weather.
3. it is obvious who or what does/did something:
   The film **will be shot** in Brazil.

We can use *by* + person/thing to show who does/did the action if this is important information:
This song **was written** by Chris Martin.

Verbs with two objects in the passive
There are two ways of making the passive of verbs that take two objects (e.g. *give, show, tell*):
The boy band **was given** first prize.
First prize **was given** to the boy band.

have something done
We use the structure *have* + thing/person + past participle when someone else does something for us:
She **had** her hair and make-up **done** before going on the stage.

Linking words and phrases

We use *in spite of, despite, although, even though, but, however* and *while* to contrast two ideas or events. *Despite* and *in spite of* are prepositions; they are followed by *-ing*, a noun or by *the fact that* + subject + verb:
The singer finished the show **despite having** a sore throat.
They continued filming **despite the bad weather**.
The concert was a success **in spite of the fact that** the guitarist was new.

Although and *even though* are conjunctions; they are followed by a noun/pronoun and a verb:
They continued filming **although / even though** the weather was bad.
She never sings her own songs **although / even though** she's written a lot.

But and *however* have the same meaning. *But* joins two halves of a sentence. *However* contrasts two separate sentences and is more formal than *but*:
Johnny Depp is a really good actor **but** I didn't enjoy his latest film.
Johnny Depp is a really good actor. **However,** I didn't enjoy his latest film.
Johnny Depp is a really good actor. I didn't, **however,** enjoy his latest film.

While can go at the beginning or in the middle of a sentence:
While I know he's a very good writer, I still don't like his books.
Annie has dark hair and eyes **while** her brother has fair hair and blue eyes.

Unit 4

Modal verbs

Obligation
We can often use either *must* or *have to* with the same meaning:
> I **must / have to phone** my mum now.

We use *must* to give orders or strong advice, including to ourselves:
> I **must remember** to bring my football boots tomorrow.
> You **must** try harder.

When there is a rule or where the obligation does not come from the speaker, *must* is possible but *have to* is more usual:
> We **have to be** at football practice early tomorrow.

We normally use *have to* for habits:
> I **have to practise** every day.

We only use *must* in the present tense. In all other tenses, we use *have to*:
> I **had to buy** new football boots because my feet had grown.
> We**'ll have to find** a new goalkeeper because Matt is ill.

Although *must* and *have to* both express obligation, *mustn't* and *don't have to* have different meanings:
> You **mustn't wear** shoes in the gym. (Don't do it.)

We also say *You can't* or *You're not allowed to*.
We use *don't have to* when there is **no** obligation to do something:
> I **don't have to take** any money because the bus is free. (It's not necessary to do it.)

We can also say *You don't need to* or *You needn't*.

Permission and advice
We use *can* to mean 'it is possible' or 'it is allowed':
> You **can borrow** my tennis racket if you want.

When we are talking about the right thing to do, we use *should(n't)* or *ought (not) to*:
> You **should tell** your parents where you are going.

Expectations
When we expect something to happen, we use *should (not)*:
> Our team **should do** well today as we've practised so much.

We also use *should* when we discover a situation is not as we expected it:
> My phone **should be** in my pocket because that's where I left it.

In the past, we say *should(n't) have*:
> We **should have scored** more goals as we had lots of chances.

Ability
We use *can* or *be able to* to say someone has an ability:
> My brother **can** cook but he's very bad at washing up.

We use *could* or *was able to* to say someone had an ability:
> I **could speak** two languages when I was little.

In all other tenses, we use a form of *be able to* to talk about ability:
> I **won't be able to come** skiing because I've hurt my foot.

Certainty and possibility
In the present we use:
1. *must* when we are sure something is true:
   > Those boots **must belong** to Cameron. He's got big feet.
2. *can't/couldn't* when we are sure something is not true:
   > That **can't be** Sara because she doesn't come to this school any more.
3. *might/may/could* when we think something is possible:
   > This text **might be** from Dan but it doesn't say.
4. *might not/may not* when we think something is uncertain:
   > I'll phone him but he **might not be** there.

Could means the same as *may/might* (something is possible) but *couldn't* means something is not true, which is different from *may not / might not* (something is uncertain).

In the past we use:
1. *must have* when we are sure something is true:
   > Ava's coat isn't here so she **must have gone** home.
2. *can't/couldn't have* when we are sure something is not true:
   > Claire's coat is here so she **can't/couldn't have gone** home.
3. *might/may/could have* when we think something is possible:
   > Adam **might have borrowed** my bike because it's not here and his is broken.
   > Luca isn't here. He **might/may/could have forgotten** to come because we changed the day.
4. *might/may not have* when we think something is uncertain:
   > You **might/may not have heard** Ellie's good news because you weren't here yesterday.

Could have means the same as *may/might have* (something is possible) but *couldn't have* means something is not true, which is different from *may/might not have* (something is uncertain).

Unit 5

Conditionals

- *If* + present simple, + present simple

We use the zero conditional to state general facts and truths:

> Children **do** better at school **if** they **sleep** well. (This is a known fact.)
> **If** children **sleep** well, they **do** better at school.

- *If* + present simple, + *will*/modal + infinitive

We use the first conditional for a future condition which we believe is possible or likely:

> **If** you **give** me some money, I**'ll** buy a ticket for you.
> **If** you **chat** to your friends during lessons, you **won't learn** anything.
> I **can** cycle to school tomorrow **if I feel** better. (I think I will feel better.)

- *If* + past simple, + *would/could* + infinitive

We use the second conditional for an imaginary condition which we believe to be impossible or unlikely. We use the past tense although the speaker is thinking about the present or the future:

> You **could win** first prize **if** you **practised** more.
> I **could reach** that shelf if I **were** taller. (But I'm not taller so I can't reach.)

! We can use *were* or *was* after *if I/he/she/it*.

Compare the first and second conditionals:

> **If** you **spent** more time on your homework, you **would get** better marks. (But you almost certainly won't spend more time.)
> **If** you **spend** more time on your homework, you**'ll get** better marks. (more likely)

- *If* + past perfect, + *would/could/might have* + past participle

We use the third conditional to talk about past events which cannot be changed, so we know the condition is impossible:

> If my dad **hadn't driven** me to school, I **would have been** late. (But he drove me so I wasn't late.)
> My friend **would have been** upset if I**'d forgotten** her birthday. (But she wasn't upset because I didn't forget.)

We sometimes see sentences which contain a mixture of second and third conditionals because of their context:

> I **wouldn't have lost** my purse **if** I **were** more careful. (I did lose it because I am generally not very careful.)
> Compare: I **wouldn't have lost** my purse if I **had been** more careful. (On this particular occasion I wasn't careful.)

We can start conditional sentences with either the *if*-clause or the main clause. If we put the main clause first, there is no comma between the clauses:

> If you smiled more, you'd make friends.
> You'd make friends if you smiled more.

Other ways of expressing *if*

Unless, in case, as/so long as, provided (that) / providing (that)

All these expressions are followed by the present tense even when we are talking about the future.

1 *Unless* means 'except if':
> You'll get a ticket if you get in the queue early. = You won't get a ticket **unless** you get in the queue early.

2 We use *in case* when we do something because something else might happen:
> I'll tidy my room **in case** my friends want to go in there. (I'll tidy it now before they come because they might want to go in there.)

In case doesn't have the same meaning as *if*:
> I'll tidy my room **if** my friends want to go in there. (I won't tidy it before they come because they might not want to go in there.)

3 *As/so long as* and *provided (that) / providing (that)* can be used instead of *if* and mean 'only if' or 'on the condition that':
> I'll go to the party **as/so long as** you come too.

I wish

To say we would like a present situation to be different, we use *I wish / if only* + past simple:

> I wish I had my own bedroom. (But I don't.)

To say we want something to happen or someone (not) to do something, we use *I wish / if only* + *would* + infinitive:

If only the rain would stop.

> I wish my mum **would let** me stay up later.

To express a wish or regret about the past we use *I wish / If only* + past perfect (it's like a third conditional):

> My mum wishes she **hadn't bought** this car. (Because it goes wrong all the time.)

Unit 6

Countable and uncountable nouns

Nouns can be either countable, e.g. *bed, child, trip* or uncountable, e.g. *accommodation, advice, experience, homework, information, music, news, pollution.*
Some nouns can be both but with different meanings:
These maths exercises are easy. [C]
Exercise is good for you. [U]

Countable nouns
1. can be singular and have *a/an* before them: *a cat, a job, an adventure*
2. can be plural (sometimes with *many/few/some* or a number before them): *some friends, many animals, three buses*

Uncountable nouns
1. cannot be plural: *Take my advice.* (**not** *advices*)
2. take a singular verb: *This food **is** delicious.*
3. can have *some/much/little* before them: *some bread, not much information, a little homework.*
4. can use other words to refer to quantity: *a slice of bread, a piece of paper*

Articles

A(n), the and no article

A(n) is used with singular countable nouns and introduces a new item of information:
*I have **an** idea.*
The is used with countable and uncountable nouns, for items mentioned before or when the speaker and listener both know what they are talking about:
*There's **a** mouse in **the** kitchen.* (The mouse is new but the speaker and listener know which kitchen.)
We don't use an article with plural countable and uncountable nouns when we talk about things in a general sense. Compare:
Musicians *don't earn much.* (musicians in general)
Music *makes people feel better.* (music in general)
The music *is too loud.* (this particular music which is playing now)

Special uses of articles

The is used with:
- oceans, seas and rivers (*the Black Sea, the Thames*)
- regions (*the south of France, the Far East*)
- groups of islands (*the Philippines*)
- names of countries that include a word like *Republic, Kingdom* or *States* (*the United States*)
- deserts and mountain ranges (*the Alps, the Kalahari Desert*).

We don't use *the* with:
- lakes (*Lake Garda*)
- continents, most countries, states, cities, towns and villages (*Europe, Florida, Rome*)
- buildings and locations which use a name (*John Lennon Airport, Edinburgh University*)
- many common expressions: *by train/bus, at home, at work, in hospital, have lunch/dinner, watch television* (but *listen to the radio*).

So and such (a/an)

So and *such* are used for emphasis, often with a result clause.
So is followed by
1. an adjective: *Global warming is **so worrying**.*
*The giraffes were **so tall** that you could see them above the trees.*
2. an adverb: *The lion came **so close** (that) everyone was scared.*
3. *much, many* and *few* with or without a noun:
*There were **so many people** (that) we couldn't see.*
*I ate **so much** (that) I could hardly move.*

Such is followed by
1. *a/an* (+ adjective) + singular noun: *It was **such a good film** (that) I wanted to watch it again.*
*I had **such a surprise** when the doorbell rang.*
2. (adjective +) plural noun: *There were **such problems** (that) we had to cancel the trip.*
*I had **such good results** in the test (that) my parents gave me a laptop.*
3. (adjective +) uncountable noun: *The trip was **such fun**.*
*This is **such strong glass** (that) it will never break.*
4. *a lot / a lot of* + noun: *There was **such a lot** to tell my mum (that) I didn't know where to start.*
*My uncle has **such a lot of money** (that) he doesn't know what to spend it on.*

Enough and too

Enough means 'sufficient, the right quantity' and *too* means 'more than enough'. We use *too* and *enough* with adjectives, adverbs and nouns.
Enough goes
1. before a noun: *I've got **enough money**.*
2. after an adjective: *I'm not **old enough** to drive.*
3. after an adverb: *We didn't run **quickly enough**.*

Too goes
1. before *much/many* + a noun: *I've got **too much** homework.*
2. before an adjective: *I'm **too young** to drive.*
3. before an adverb: *He ran **too quickly** for us to catch him.*

GRAMMAR REFERENCE 83

Unit 7

Verbs and expressions followed by *to* or *-ing*

- Verb + *to* + infinitive, e.g. (*can't*) *afford, agree, aim, appear, arrange, attempt, decide, demand, deserve, fail, forget, hope, learn, manage, offer, plan, pretend, refuse, seem, tend,* (*can't*) *wait*:
  You **deserve to do** well.
  She **pretended not to notice**.

- Verb (+ object) + *to* + infinitive, e.g. *ask, choose, expect, help, intend, prepare, promise, want*:
  We **expected** them **to wait** for us.

- Verb + object + *to* + infinitive, e.g. *dare, encourage, force, invite, order, persuade, remind, teach, tell, warn*:
  My friend **dared** me **to jump** across the river.

- *Make* and *let* are followed by the infinitive without *to* and always have an object:
  I **made** my brother **come** shopping with me.

- Verbs followed by *-ing*, e.g. *avoid, can't help, can't stand, carry on, consider, delay, dislike, enjoy, feel like, finish, give up, imagine, involve, keep/keep on, mention,* (*not*) *mind, miss, postpone, practise, put off, suggest*:
  I **suggested playing** badminton instead of tennis.
  I **enjoy not having** much to do on Sundays.

- Verbs and expressions ending in a preposition always take *-ing*:
  I **gave up doing** gymnastics when I hurt my foot.
  I am **interested in becoming** a fashion designer.

- Some verbs are followed by either the *to*-infinitive or *-ing* with little or no difference in meaning, e.g. *attempt, begin, can't bear, continue, hate, like, love, prefer, propose, start*:
  I **prefer to shop** / I **prefer shopping** at the market.
  ! *Would like, would prefer* and *would love* are always followed by the *to*-infinitive.

- Some verbs can be followed by the *to*-infinitive or *-ing* but with a difference in meaning, e.g. *remember, forget, mean, go on, try, stop*:
  Remember to take your keys with you. (something you have to do)
  I **remember taking** my keys with me. (a memory of a past action)
  Try to walk faster. (attempt to do it if you can)
  Try taking more exercise. (a suggestion or experiment)

Reported speech

Tenses

When we report what someone else said (direct speech, e.g. *I am cold*), we are usually reporting some time after the actual speech, so we change the tenses used by the original speaker (reported speech, e.g. *He said he was cold.*).

direct speech	→	reported speech
present simple	→	past simple
present continuous	→	past continuous
will	→	would
is/am/are going to	→	was/were going to
past simple	→	past perfect
past continuous	→	past perfect continuous
present perfect	→	past perfect
can/may/might	→	could

If the verb in direct speech is past perfect, we don't change it. These verbs don't change either when they are reported: *could, would, might, ought to* and *used to*.
! When we report *must*, we usually use *had to*:
  '*I must buy* some new trainers.' → She said she **had to buy** some new trainers.
but we use *must* not *had to* when we report a negative or a deduction:
  '*You mustn't tell Sam.*' → She said we mustn't tell Sam.
  '*Giulia must be tired.*' → She said that Giulia must be tired.

Say and tell

We often use *say* and *tell* to report speech:
  He **said** (that) he would be late.
  He **said to me** (that) he would be late. (not *He said me....*)
  He **told me** (that) he would be late. (not *He told to me....* or *He told that....*)
Other common reporting verbs are *add, agree, answer, explain* and *reply*. The *to* infinitive is usually used after them: *He promised/agreed to be quiet*.

Reporting questions

When we report questions we don't use the question form of the verb and there is no question mark. Questions with question words (*who, what, how*, etc.) keep the question words when reported:
  How do you feel? → Peter asked Tom how he felt. (**not** *Peter asked Tom how did he feel.*)
Questions we can answer with *yes* or *no* are reported with *if* or *whether*:
  '*Do you like my new shoes?*' → Rachel asked Tom **if/whether** he liked her new shoes.

GRAMMAR REFERENCE

Unit 8

Relative clauses

We use *which*, *who*, *where* or *whose* to join two ideas about a thing or things.

This is my camera. I had it for my birthday. It has stopped working.
→ *This camera, **which** I had for my birthday, has stopped working.* (**not** ~~which I had it for my birthday~~ – We use *which* instead of *it*.)
*The pool **where** we usually swim is closed today.*

- There are two kinds of relative clauses: defining and non-defining.

Defining clauses tell us essential information about the things or people they refer to:
The girl who won the competition lives next door to me. (If we remove the underlined words, we don't know which girl is being described.)
The shop where I bought this laptop has a sale. (If we remove the underlined words, we don't know which shop.)
The boy whose father owns the garage sold me his bicycle. (If we remove the underlined words, we don't know which boy.)

- Non-defining relative clauses tell us extra information about the things or people they refer to:
My brother, who is three years older than me, won a competition yesterday.
My bicycle, which I haven't had very long, is too small for me.
The important information is about the competition / size of the bicycle and the underlined words are extra information – we don't need them.

Defining relative clauses

1. are never separated from the rest of the sentence by commas:
   The bag which I left on the bus was never found.
2. often use *that* instead of *who* or *which*:
   *Who is the girl **that** you were talking to?*
   *There's a new shop in the village **that** sells computer games.*
3. often omit the relative pronoun if it is the object of the verb in the relative clause:
   *The programme about famous scientists (**which**/**that**) I saw last night was really interesting.* (The relative clause begins with a new subject (*I*) so we can omit *which/that*.)
   We can say:
   The bus that I usually catch to school didn't come today. **or**
   The bus I usually catch to school didn't come today.
   but we keep the relative pronoun if it is the subject of the verb in the relative clause:
   The scientist who was on TV last night works with my dad. (*was* refers back to the scientist so we can't omit *who*.)
   ~~The scientist was on TV last night works with my dad.~~

Non-defining relative clauses

1. must be separated from the rest of the sentence by commas:
   Sam's granny, who lives in Switzerland, used to be a champion skier.
2. never use *that*:
   My uncle, who is an actor, often comes to stay.
   not ~~My uncle, that is an actor, often comes to stay.~~
3. never omit the relative pronoun:
   *Katya, **whose** family own a restaurant, is coming to the film with us.*
4. sometimes refer to the whole of the main clause:
   My cousins in Canada have invited me to spend the summer with them, which is really fantastic! (The idea of spending the summer in Canada is fantastic.)

Prepositions in relative clauses

In informal sentences, we put the preposition at the end.
That's my sister. The teacher is talking to her.
→ *That's my sister **who** the teacher is talking **to**.*
Peter had a party. He invited me to it. It was very good.
→ *Peter's party, **which** he invited me **to**, was very good.*
If the sentence is very formal, we can put the preposition before the relative pronoun.
*We will address the problem **to which** you refer at the school council meeting.*

WRITING GUIDE

This guide will help you prepare for Writing, Paper 2 of *Cambridge English: First for Schools*. The practice tasks and model answers will help you to see what is expected and what makes a good answer to the writing tasks.

Planning and timing

There are two parts to the writing paper, which lasts one hour and 20 minutes.

Writing Part 1
- This is compulsory. You have to write 140–190 words.
- In Part 1 you are guided through the task by the instructions and notes.
- Allow five minutes for reading and planning, and 25–30 minutes for writing.

Writing Part 2
- This has a choice of four questions. You have to write **one** answer of 140–190 words.
- In Part 2 you have to choose your question, and then plan it yourself.
- Allow five minutes for choosing your question and planning it, and 30 minutes for writing.

Leave ten minutes at the end of the exam for checking the grammar, spelling and punctuation of your work.

Writing Part 1

Essay

(See Unit 1 page 12 and Unit 8 page 64.)

Essays **always** ask you to give your opinion, and you will need to give examples to support your ideas and to explain why you hold these views. There will be two notes given with ideas that you must write about, and you have to think of a third idea for yourself. You may disagree with a statement you are asked to discuss and have to give reasons for your disagreement. You will be able to answer the question from your own knowledge and experience. No specialised knowledge is required.

Practice task and model answer

1 Read the exam question below and underline the important words. Then answer the questions.

   1 Who is the essay for?
   2 Do you have to write about both languages and science subjects?
   3 Should you write about any other subjects?
   4 Can you say anything you like in the conclusion?

In your English class you have been talking about school subjects. Now your English teacher has asked you to write an essay for homework.

Write your essay using **all** the notes and giving reasons for your point of view.

Is it more useful to study several foreign languages or to study several science subjects at school?

Notes
Write about:

1. what is more useful
2. what is easier to learn
3. ………………… (your own idea)

2 Now read this candidate's answer and the points below it. Answer the questions in *italics*.

> I would like to start my essay by saying that whether languages or sciences are more useful depends very much on what job you would like to do. If you want to be a doctor, or a great inventor, of course you will need to study science subjects. However, I would argue that there really isn't much point in studying science subjects if you are going to be a history teacher, or work in a shop.
>
> On the other hand, learning languages is always useful, whatever career you want to have in the future. Of course, English is very useful because so many people speak it, but other languages, like Spanish and Chinese, are also very important.
>
> I think that it is good to study both sciences and languages if you can, but not many people will become experts in science. That is because for most people, science beyond a certain level is far too difficult, although it's good to have a basic knowledge.
>
> Therefore, I would like to conclude by saying that, ideally, everyone should study several foreign languages, simply because they are useful in every job.
> [188 words]

This is a good answer because:
- the candidate has answered the question well, talking about both science subjects and foreign languages.
- the two points are covered. *Where? What was the candidate's opinion?*
- there is a clear third point. *Where? What does the candidate say?*
- the candidate has come to a definite conclusion. *What is it?*
- it is well organised into paragraphs. *How? Write the candidate's plan.*
- it is easy to read and well-linked. *Underline the linking phrases.*

Writing Part 2

You have a choice of four questions in Part 2 and you only have to answer one of them. Questions 2, 3 and 4 will be three of these: story, review, article, informal letter or email.

Question 5 will be on the chosen set text. This may be in the form of an essay, article, letter or review. You should only attempt Question 5 if you have studied the relevant book.

Choosing your question and planning your answer

Read through the questions and decide which one you want to answer.

Avoid a question if:
- you don't understand it, or are unsure about what you must do.
- you don't have the necessary vocabulary.
- you don't have enough ideas to write about.

When you have chosen the question:
- underline the important words in it.
- get your ideas together and make a plan. You can do this as a map or diagram, or simply a list of points. There is an example of this on page 64.
- do not start writing until you have a clear plan to work from.

Story

(See Unit 2 page 20.)

Practice task and model answer

1 Read the exam question on page 88 and underline the important words. Then answer the questions.

1. Who is the story for? Where will it be read?
2. Over what period of time does the story take place?
3. Do the events in the story have to be positive? Were they planned or not?

WRITING GUIDE 87

> Your English teacher has asked you to write a story for the school website.
> Your story must **begin** with this sentence:
> *I was expecting to have a quiet day, but it turned out to be just the opposite.*
> Your story must include:
> - a robbery
> - a phone call
>
> Write your **story**.

2   Now read this candidate's answer and the points below it. Answer the questions in italics.

> **How we became local heroes**
> I was expecting to have a quiet day, but it turned out to be just the opposite. It was Saturday morning and I was reading sleepily when the phone rang. 'Come quickly, Sam, I need your help!' It was my best friend George, so I couldn't refuse. 'Where are you?' I asked. 'I'm at home, watching the house opposite through my binoculars. Come quickly, through the back garden.'
>
> I rushed round. George told me there was a robbery going on. A large van had driven up and the TV and all the computers were being removed. 'But George, there's a much simpler explanation,' I said impatiently. 'They must be moving house.' 'Don't be silly! You know Simon's in our class. He would have said something if his family had been moving!' I realised he was right.
>
> So we phoned the police, who arrived very rapidly. Simon's parents were so relieved and happy that we had stopped the burglary that they took us out for a pizza that night. And by Monday we were famous, because our picture appeared in the paper under the heading 'Local heroes!'. [188 words]

This is a good answer because:
- the story follows well from the prompt sentence, and it is easy to follow what happens.
- the candidate has included the two essential points. *Where? Underline them.*
- it is clearly paragraphed and well punctuated.
- the candidate has used several different past tenses very effectively. *Which ones? Underline an example of each tense.*
- the story contains some direct speech. *Highlight it. Who is speaking and why is it effective here?*
- the candidate has used a good range of vocabulary and expressions. *Underline some that you think are effective.*
- the candidate has given the story a title. *Why?*

Review

(See Unit 3 page 23.)
Reviews may be on a wide range of topics, and not just on films or books.

Practice task and model answer

1   Read the exam question below and underline the important words. Then answer the questions.

1   Who is the review for?
2   Where will it be read?
3   What sort of website do you have to write about?
4   Do you have to recommend it?

> You have seen this notice in an English-language magazine for teenagers.
>
> **Reviews wanted!**
> **My favourite website**
> Have you got a favourite website that you spend a lot of time on?
>
> Write us a review of it. Describe the website, explain why you spend a lot of time on it and say whether you would recommend it to other people.
>
> The best reviews will appear in the magazine next month.

Write your **review**.

2   Now read this candidate's answer and the points below it. Answer the questions in *italics*.

> My favourite website
> The best website I have been on is ultimateguitar.com. I spend lots of time on it because I'm learning to play the electric guitar and everything I need is on this site.
>
> It has reviews of all kinds of guitar music, which means jazz and classical as well as pop, rock and so on, so there is something for different tastes. In addition, there is always news and gossip about well-known guitarists. And better still, there are really good interviews to watch, with rock stars, classical guitarists and so on.
>
> However, the most fantastic thing about the site is that you can download tabs for all your favourite guitar music from it. It has all the famous riffs and they add new music every week. It's such a popular feature that there is sometimes a queue for downloading. I set it up before school, so it's there when I get home.
>
> I love this website, and I would recommend it to other guitar fans, especially if they are players themselves. And even if you don't play, I'm sure you will find it interesting! [184 words]

WRITING GUIDE

This is a good answer because:
- the candidate has dealt with all the points, giving a clear description of the website and recommending it.
- it is well organised and clearly divided into paragraphs.
- it is well-linked. *Underline the linking words and phrases.*
- it contains different verb tenses. *Which tense is mostly used in the answer? Find examples of any other tenses.*
- it contains a good range of vocabulary about music and websites. *Highlight some.*

Letter and email

(See Unit 4 page 36 and Unit 7 page 57.)
Letters and emails often ask you to give information and opinions to a friend who is doing a project or wants advice. You should not write a long introduction with lots of news and chat, but go straight into the main topic. There are usually several pieces of information to provide, or several questions to answer. The topic will be something connected to your knowledge of your own country and/or personal experience. No specialised knowledge is required.

Practice task and model answer

1 Read the exam question below and underline the important words. Then answer the questions.

   1 Who is going to read your letter?
   2 Can you write about any city?
   3 You have to write about the history of the city. Can you write about anything else?

> You have received a letter from your English friend Hannah.
>
> > We're doing a project on capital cities in my history class. Could you write and tell me something about your capital city and its history and what you would recommend a tourist from another country to visit?
> >
> > Thanks a lot – and write soon.
> >
> > Best wishes, Hannah
>
> Write your **letter**.

2 Now read this candidate's answer and the points below it. Answer the questions in italics.

> Dear Hannah,
> Your history project sounds fascinating!
>
> Paris has a long and interesting history, going back to Roman times. The oldest part is the Ile de la Cité, where the Romans first settled, and then the French kings built the Sainte-Chappelle, the Conciergerie prison and the wonderful cathedral of Notre Dame there a thousand years later. These monuments are still there, but in the nineteenth century a famous architect called Baron Haussmann pulled down many of the houses around them to make way for new buildings, which everyone now thinks of as being typical of Paris.
>
> I think the one place a tourist should see is the Louvre. Before the French Revolution it was a royal palace; it's a fantastic building, and it contains the famous picture of the Mona Lisa, and wonderful statues. The Louvre is enormous; there is too much to see in a lifetime!
>
> Sightseeing is tiring, so I would suggest visiting the Latin Quarter, the student area where there are lots of little restaurants, or going for a walk by the beautiful River Seine and admiring the views of the Eiffel Tower.
> Best wishes,
> Andrea
> [189 words]

This is a good answer because:
- the candidate has answered the question well, writing in an interesting way about the capital city, its history and places to visit. *Underline the historical facts mentioned and highlight the places you can visit.*
- the letter is well organised and divided into paragraphs, and sentences are well structured.
- the candidate has started and ended the letter with friendly phrases. *Underline them.*

3 Here are some phrases you may find useful in a letter or email.

Write the headings below into the correct box.

Apologising   Asking questions   Giving reasons
Making requests and offers   ~~Responding positively~~
Stating opinion or preference
Suggesting and recommending   Thanking

Purpose	Phrases to use
Responding positively	What a fantastic idea! It's great you can … I was pleased to hear that …
	Thanks for agreeing to … Thank you very much for … Thanks for inviting me to …
	In my opinion/view For me, / As for me, I think / believe / feel that … I'd prefer to … / I'd rather … I prefer -ing to -ing It would be better to … than to …
	I suggest …-ing. Why don't you …? How about …-ing? You could always … Why not try …-ing? I'd recommend …-ing.
	I'd … if I were you, since I think it will be interesting / great fun / enjoyable. The best thing to do is … because … The best reason for doing this is that …
	I'm really sorry but … Sorry for (not) …-ing before but … I'd like to apologise for (not) …-ing.
	Do you think you could …? Could you possibly …? Could you …, please? I could … if you'd like me to. Can I … for you? Shall I …? Would you like me to …?
	Can you …? Do you …? Do you think you could/should …? Do you have to …? Do you know if / whether / when …? Can you tell me if / whether / when …?

Beginning and ending a letter or email

You can begin and end emails and letters in a similar way.

Informal style: writing to a close friend, another young person, or a member of your family
Begin with: *Hello, Hi* or *Dear* + first name.
End with: *Best wishes, All the best, Love*

More formal style: writing to an older person or someone you don't know well
Begin with: *Dear* + first name or *Dear Mr/ Mrs/Miss* + surname
End with: *Yours, With kind regards* or *Yours sincerely*

Here are some phrases to **start** your email/ letter:
Informal: *Great news/idea/plan! I'm really pleased for you! It was great to hear from you.*
More formal: *I was pleased to receive your email/letter about …*

Some phrases to **end** your letter/email:
Informal: *I've got to dash now. / That's all for now. / Write soon. / Looking forward to seeing you soon.*
More formal: *I look forward to hearing from you again/soon. / Give my best wishes to your family.*

Article

(See Unit 6 page 49.)
Articles can be on a very wide range of topics, and can include some that are not found in other question types. However, you will also find articles on topics that you do find in other question types, for example, sport, friends or food. Try to engage the interest of your reader and write in a lively style. Where appropriate, you can include questions and amusing comments if you wish.

Practice task and model answer

1 Read the exam question below and underline the important words. Then answer the questions.

1 Where will the article appear?
2 Who will read it?
3 Do you have to use the three suggestions?

You see this announcement in an international teenage magazine.

> **Articles wanted!**
>
> **The Moon**
>
> Beautiful evenings? Space travel?
> Poems and songs?
> What does the Moon mean to you?
> Write us an article explaining what you feel about the Moon and why.
> The best articles will be published in the magazine next month.

Write your **article**.

2 Now read this candidate's answer and the points below it. Answer the questions in italics.

What the Moon means to me …

The Moon has been important to humans since prehistoric times. I spend hours looking at the night sky, the Moon, and the stars. I love the Moon, especially when it is full and bright. That's not because I believe in vampires and other scary things that are supposed to appear when the Moon is full, but because it is one of the most beautiful things I've ever seen! That is what the Moon means to me – beauty.

Looking at the Moon also makes me think about the astronauts who landed there in the 1960s, so the Moon connects me to space travel and scientific progress. I have even read science fiction stories about humans living on the Moon, but how would we breathe? We would have to live in an artificial atmosphere, which would be horrible.

Finally, the Moon also reminds me of childhood stories. There were often pictures of the Moon in them, with cute little animals looking up at it! Now I'm older, I've heard all the old songs about the Moon, and love and romance, and of course I've read poems about it too ….

[189 words]

This is a good answer because:
- the candidate has answered the question well, using some of the suggestions.
- it is well planned and divided into paragraphs. *How? Write the candidate's plan.*
- it contains different verb tenses. *Underline an example of each one.*

Set text

(See Unit 5 page 45.)
There is one question on the set text. You must answer the question from your knowledge of the book. For this question you need knowledge of the main characters in the book and the main events. You may be asked to write an essay, article, letter, or review, although essays are the most common.

The book title changes every two years, and information can be found on the Cambridge English website (www.cambridgeenglish.org).

Here are two examples of set text questions and candidate answers. Read the example question and candidate answer. Has the candidate answered the question?

Great Expectations by Charles Dickens

> You have seen the following announcement in an international school magazine. You have decided to write an article about a strange character in *Great Expectations*.
>
> **Articles wanted**
> Tell us about a strange character in a book you know.
> – What did this person look like?
> – How did this person behave?
> – Why was this person so strange?
> The best articles will be published in the magazine.
>
> Write your **article** about a strange character in *Great Expectations*.

WRITING GUIDE 91

Candidate answer (corrected)

Are you looking for stories with strange characters? Then you must read Great Expectations by Charles Dickens. I read it recently and I was particularly interested in one of the female characters, an old lady called Miss Havisham.

Wearing her old wedding dress, which has turned yellow, Miss Havisham spends her days in her room with everything prepared as if she is going to get married. The strange thing is that she was supposed to get married many years ago, but when the groom stood her up in church on her wedding day, she stopped every clock in her house and left everything as it was at that moment.

This lady is not only strange because of the way she dresses but also because of her bad temper and unusual behaviour. She has always taught her adopted daughter, Estella, to take revenge on the male sex and she enjoys watching her breaking men's hearts. Although she is full of hatred, we should feel sorry for Miss Havisham since her behaviour can be justified by her sad past.

[177 words]

This is a good answer because it addresses the three parts of the question in a clear and straightforward way. The candidate catches the reader's attention by asking a question at the start of the article and answering it.

How does the candidate describe Miss Havisham?
Appearance:
Behaviour:
What reason does she give to explain why Miss Havisham is so strange?

Phantom of the Opera by Gaston Leroux

Your English teacher has asked you to write an essay for homework answering this question:

Who was the Phantom of the Opera and what do you learn in the story about his childhood and his past?

Candidate answer (corrected)

The Phantom of the Opera was in fact a normal person like anyone else; the only difference was that he was ugly, and so he hid from the world. The Phantom of the Opera is believed to be a ghost in the Opera House that haunts everybody and might even sometimes kill. However, the Phantom is in fact a real person called Erik, who fell in love with a singer at the Opera House, a girl called Christine Daaé. Erik taught Christine to sing and had expected her love in return.

Erik, the Phantom of the Opera, had a very sad and lonely life. He was born in a village to a very poor family. Unfortunately, when he was born, his mother hated Erik because of his ugly face and eventually she forced him to wear a mask.

Because of this, Erik left home and travelled to different places. He had the mind of a genius, and he was a brilliant architect. His final stop was when he started building the Opera House. He designed it to his advantage, building many secret passages and also a house on the lake; he hoped Christine would live with him there.

[198 words]

This is a good answer because
- it addresses both parts of the question in a clear and straightforward way. *What was the candidate's plan for the essay?*
- It only describes those parts of the plot of the book that are relevant to the question. *Underline them.*

IRREGULAR VERBS

verb	past simple	past participle	verb	past simple	past participle
arise	arose	arisen	hear	heard	heard
be	was/were	been	hide	hid	hidden
beat	beat	beaten	hit	hit	hit
become	became	become	hold	held	held
begin	began	begun	hurt	hurt	hurt
bend	bent	bent	keep	kept	kept
bite	bit	bitten	kneel	knelt	knelt
bleed	bled	bled	know	knew	known
blow	blew	blown	lay	laid	laid
break	broke	broken	lead	led	led
bring	brought	brought	lean	leant/ leaned	leant/ leaned
broadcast	broadcast	broadcast	learn	learnt/ learned	learnt/ learned
build	built	built			
burn	burnt/ burned	burnt/ burned	leave	left	left
burst	burst	burst	lend	lent	lent
buy	bought	bought	let	let	let
catch	caught	caught	lie	lay	lain
choose	chose	chosen	light	lit	lit
come	came	come	lose	lost	lost
cost	cost	cost	make	made	made
creep	crept	crept	mean	meant	meant
cut	cut	cut	meet	met	met
deal	dealt	dealt	pay	paid	paid
dig	dug	dug	put	put	put
do	did	done	read	read	read
draw	drew	drawn	ride	rode	ridden
dream	dreamt/ dreamed	dreamt/ dreamed	ring	rang	rung
			rise	rose	risen
drink	drank	drunk	run	ran	run
drive	drove	driven	say	said	said
eat	ate	eaten	see	saw	seen
fall	fell	fallen	sell	sold	sold
feed	fed	fed	send	sent	sent
feel	felt	felt	set	set	set
fight	fought	fought	sew	sewed	sewn
find	found	found	shake	shook	shaken
fly	flew	flown	shine	shone	shone
forbid	forbade	forbidden	shoot	shot	shot
forget	forgot	forgotten	show	showed	shown
forgive	forgave	forgiven	shrink	shrank	shrunk
freeze	froze	frozen	shut	shut	shut
get	got	got	sing	sang	sung
give	gave	given	sink	sank	sunk
go	went	gone/been	sit	sat	sat
grow	grew	grown	sleep	slept	slept
hang	hung	hung	slide	slid	slid
have	had	had	smell	smelt/ smelled	smelt/ smelled

verb	past simple	past participle
sow	sowed	sown
speak	spoke	spoken
spell	spelt/ spelled	spelt/ spelled
spend	spent	spent
spill	spilt/ spilled	spilt/ spilled
spit	spat	spat
split	split	split
spoil	spoilt/ spoiled	spoilt/ spoiled
spread	spread	spread
spring	sprang	sprung
stand	stood	stood
steal	stole	stolen
stick	stuck	stuck
sting	stung	stung
strike	struck	struck
swear	swore	sworn
sweep	swept	swept
swell	swelled	swollen
swim	swam	swum
swing	swung	swung
take	took	taken
teach	taught	taught
tear	tore	torn
tell	told	told
think	thought	thought
throw	threw	thrown
understand	understood	understood
wake	woke	woken
wear	wore	worn
weep	wept	wept
win	won	won
write	wrote	written

WORDLIST

adj = adjective, *adv* = adverb, *n* = noun, *v* = verb,
pv = phrasal verb, *prep* = preposition, *exp* = expression

Note: There is space for you to write other words you would like to learn.

Unit 1

approach *n* a way of doing something

approval *n* when you think that something or someone is good or right

arrogant *adj* believing that you are better than other people

at all *exp* in any way or of any type (used to make negatives and questions stronger)

at last *exp* finally

at least *exp* as much as, or more than, a number or amount

at once *exp* immediately

be put off *pv* to have your attention taken away from something you are doing

believe in *v* to be confident that something is effective and right

bold *adj* brave

celebrate *v* to have a party or a nice meal because it is a special day or something good has happened

community *n* the people living in a particular area

daylight *n* the natural light from the sun during the day

demand *v* a strong request or need for something

depend on *v* to need the help and support of someone or something

doubtful *adj* If you are doubtful about something, you are uncertain about it.

eager *adj* wanting to do or have something very much

energetic *adj* having or needing a lot of energy

expect (someone to do something) *v* to think that someone should behave in a particular way or do a particular thing

formal *adj* not casual, official

get away with *pv* to succeed in avoiding punishment for something

impatient *adj* If you are impatient, you get angry with people who make mistakes or you hate waiting for things.

informal *adj* suitable for when you are with friends or family, but not for official occasions

irritated *adj* annoyed

jealous *adj* not happy because you want something that someone else has

make a comparison *exp* to compare two or more things

relieved *adj* feeling happy because something bad did not happen

rely *v* to need someone or something in order to be successful

significant *adj* important

spot *n* a place

stage *n* a period of development

thrilling *adj* very exciting

tradition *n* a custom or way of behaving that has continued for a long time in a group of people

weird *adj* very strange

My words

....
....
....
....
....
....
....
....
....

Unit 2

accidental adj by chance

adventurous adj liking to try new or difficult things

aggressive adj angry and violent towards another person

attempt n when you try to do something

aware adj knowing about something

bearable adj If an unpleasant situation is bearable, you can accept or deal with it.

clumsy adj Clumsy people move in a way that is not controlled or careful, and often knock or damage things.

confidence n when you are certain of your ability to do things well

considerable adj large or important enough to have an effect

controversial adj causing a lot of disagreement or argument

courageous adj brave

decisive adj making decisions quickly and easily

desirable adj If something is desirable, it is very good or attractive and most people would want it.

disappearance n when someone or something suddenly goes somewhere and is impossible to see or find

disaster n a very bad situation, especially something that causes a lot of harm or damage

draw attention to exp to bring people's notice to something

explorer n someone who travels to places where no one has ever been in order to find out what is there

furious adj very angry

get into trouble exp to get into problems or difficulties, or to be punished for something

highlight v to emphasise something or make people notice something

hold your breath exp to stop breathing

industrial adj connected with industry

injury n damage to someone's body

isolated adj a long way from other places

judgement n the ability to form valuable opinions and make good decisions

logical adj using reason

mysterious adj strange and not explained or understood

optimistic adj always thinking that good things will happen

predictable adj happening or behaving in a way that you expect and not unusual or interesting

rapid adj happening or moving very quickly

remarkable adj very unusual in a way that you admire

rural adj relating to the countryside and not to towns

treasure n very valuable things, usually in the form of a store of precious metals, stones or money

universal adj relating to everyone in the world, or to everyone in a particular group

warning n something that tells or shows you that something bad may happen

My words

....
....
....
....
....
....
....
....
....
....

Unit 3

appeal *v* to attract or interest someone

be supposed to (do something) *v* to have to, should (do something)

cast *n* all the actors in a film or play

character *n* a person in a book, film, etc.

contain *v* If one thing contains another, it has it inside it.

costume *n* all the clothes that you wear at the same time, usually special clothes

determined *adj* wanting so much to do something that you keep trying very hard

direction *n* the control of a film, play, etc.

distinguish *v* to see or understand the differences between two people, ideas, or things

emotion *n* a strong feeling such as love or anger

exceptional *adj* very good and better than most other people or things

extend *v* to make something bigger or longer

have trouble (doing something) *exp* to experience difficulties in doing something

hero *n* the main character in a book or film

impressive *adj* Someone or something that is impressive makes you admire and respect them.

justice *n* treatment of people that is fair

lyrics *n* the words of a song

outstanding *adj* excellent and much better than most

overall *adv* in general rather than in particular

personality *n* the qualities that make one person different from another

play a part *exp* to take a role in a film, play, etc.

plot *n* the things that happen in a story

producer *n* someone who controls how a film, play, programme, or musical recording is made

reaction *n* something you say, feel, or do because of something that has happened

review *n* a piece of writing in a newspaper that gives an opinion about a new book, film, etc.

romantic comedy *n* a film which combines a comedy with a love story

schedule *n* a plan that tells you when things will happen

script *n* the words in a film, play, etc.

set *n* the place where a film or play is performed or recorded and the pictures, furniture, etc. that are used

shot *n* a short piece in a film in which there is a single action or a short series of actions

special effects *n* an unusual type of action in a film, or an entertainment on stage, created by using special equipment

stand out *pv* to be very noticeable

stunt *n* when someone does something dangerous that needs great skill, usually in a film

symbol *n* a sign or object that is used to mean something

My words

....
....
....
....
....
....
....
....
....
....

Unit 4

athletics *n* the sports which include running, jumping and throwing

(a) balanced diet *exp* a diet that contains the right amounts of different types of food

benefit *n* a helpful or good effect

benefit *v* to have a helpful or good effect on someone or something

convenience *n* when something is easy to use and suitable for what you want to do

curiosity *n* the feeling of wanting to know or learn about something

decoration *n* when you make something look more attractive by putting things on it, or something that you use to do this

defender *n* someone in a sports team who tries to prevent the other team from scoring points, goals, etc.

division *n* when something is separated into parts or groups

equality *n* when everyone is equal and has the same rights, etc.

generosity *n* the quality of being generous

get involved in *exp* to take part in something

independence *n* when someone looks after themselves and does not need help from other people

keep fit *exp* to remain healthy and strong, usually as a result of exercise

lap *n* one journey around a race track

martial arts *n* sports that are traditional Japanese or Chinese forms of fighting or defending yourself, e.g. judo, karate

opponent *n* someone who you compete against in a game or competition

patience *n* when you are able to stay calm and not get angry, especially when something takes a long time

penalty *n* in sports, an advantage given to a team when the other team has broken a rule, e.g. in football, a kick straight at the goal

pitch *n* an area of ground where a sport is played

potential *adj* A potential problem, employer, partner, etc. may become one in the future, although they are not one now.

production *n* the process of making or growing goods to be sold

professional *n* Someone is a professional if they get money for a sport or activity which most people do as a hobby.

pudding *n* in the UK, sweet food that is usually eaten as the last part of a meal

react *v* to say, do or feel something because of something else that has been said or done

referee *n* someone who makes sure that players follow the rules during a sports game

responsible (for) *adj* having control and authority over something or someone and the duty of taking care of it or them

similarity *n* when two things or people are similar, or a way in which they are similar

tackle *n* when you try to get the ball from someone in a game like football

track *n* a path, often circular, used for races

umpire *n* someone whose job is to watch a sports game and make sure that the players obey the rules

My words

....
....
....
....
....
....
....
....
....
....

Unit 5

adapt *v* to change for a new situation

appreciate *v* to feel grateful for something

canteen *n* a restaurant in an office, factory or school

capable *adj* able to do things well

combine *v* to become mixed or joined, or to mix or join things together

come across *pv* to find or meet by chance

come down with *pv* to start to suffer from an illness, especially one that is not serious

come up with *pv* to suggest or think of an idea or plan

communicative *adj* willing to talk to people and give them information

competitive *adj* wanting to win or be better than other people

construction *n* the work of building houses, offices, bridges, etc.

demanding *adj* needing a lot of your time, attention or effort

enthusiastic *adj* keen, eager, showing enthusiasm

extent *n* the size or importance of something

facilities *n* buildings or equipment that are provided for a particular purpose

give up *pv* to stop doing a particular activity or job

go off *pv* to stop liking or being interested in someone or something

go over *pv* to examine or look at something in a careful or detailed way

go through *pv* to experience a difficult or unpleasant situation

look down on *pv* to think that someone is less important than you

set *n* a group of pupils at school who have a similar level in a particular subject

shelter *n* a place that protects you from bad weather or danger

sports kit *n* the clothes that pupils wear to play sports at school

state school *n* a school that is free to go to because the government provides the money for it

(be) streamed *v* (relating to school pupils of a similar level, age and intelligence) to be grouped together

sympathetic *adj* showing that you understand and care about someone's problems

thorough *adj* careful and covering every detail

volunteer *n* someone who works without being paid, especially work that involves helping people

My words

....
....
....
....
....
....
....
....
....
....

Unit 6

air conditioning *n* a system that keeps the air cool in a building or car

be green *exp* to be interested in protecting the environment

bush *n* a short, thick plant with a lot of branches

climate change *n* the way the Earth's weather is changing

environment *n* the air, water and land in or on which people, animals and plants live

erupt *v* If a volcano erupts, it suddenly throws out fire and melted rocks.

flooding *n* when the land becomes covered with water, especially in a way that causes problems

fuel *n* a substance that is burned to give heat or power

humid *adj* Humid air or weather is hot and slightly wet.

hurricane *n* a violent storm with very strong winds

litter *n* pieces of paper and other waste that are left in public places

mild *adj* When the weather in winter is mild, it is not cold.

packaged (food) *adj* in boxes or containers to be sold

pine tree *n* an evergreen (= never losing its leaves) tree that grows in cooler areas of the world

pollution *n* damage caused to water, air, etc. by bad substances or waste

pressure *n* difficult situations that make you feel worried or unhappy

purchase *v* to buy something

rainfall *n* the amount of rain that falls in a particular place at a particular time

ready meals *n* prepared meals that are often already cooked and just need to be heated up

recycle *v* to use paper, glass, plastic, etc. again and not throw it away

rubbish *n* things that you throw away because you do not want them

shortage *n* when there is not enough of something

submit *v* to send a document, plan, etc. to someone so that they can consider it

transport *n* when people or things are moved from one place to another

volcano *n* a mountain with a large hole at the top which sometimes explodes

My words

....
....
....
....
....
....
....
....
....

Unit 7

admire *v* to like or respect someone or something because they are good or clever

amused *adj* showing that you think something is funny

ashamed *adj* feeling bad because you have done something wrong

be keen on *exp* to be very interested in something

belief *n* when you believe that something is true or real

can't bear *exp* to strongly dislike someone or something

casual *adj* Casual clothes are comfortable and not formal.

(feel) cheated *exp* to feel that you have been prevented from obtaining or achieving something

concerned *adj* worried

conventional *adj* Conventional objects or ways of doing things are the usual ones which have been used for a long time.

deliberate *adj* If an action is deliberate, you wanted or planned to do it.

discouraged *adj* having lost your confidence in something or your enthusiasm for it

drag *v* to pull something or someone somewhere, usually with difficulty

elegant *adj* stylish and attractive

expectation *n* when you expect something to happen (often something good)

fate *n* what happens to a particular person or thing, especially something negative

freedom *n* the right to live in the way you want without being controlled by anyone else

gaze *n* a long look at someone or something

keep up with *pv* If you keep up with something or someone, you stay at the same level as it or them.

on the other hand *exp* (usually following *on the one hand*) used to compare two different facts or opinions on a situation

outrageous *adj* shocking or extreme

passionate *adj* showing a strong feeling about a subject

second-hand *adj* If something is second-hand, someone else had it or used it before you.

shocking *adj* very bad and making you feel upset

show off *pv* to behave in a way that is intended to attract attention

take no notice of *exp* not to give attention to someone or something

taste *n* particular things you like, such as styles of music, clothes, decoration, etc.

upset *adj* sad or worried because something bad has happened

vintage *adj* having all the best or most typical qualities of something, especially from the past

whereas *conj* compared with the fact that

My words

………………………………………………………………
………………………………………………………………
………………………………………………………………
………………………………………………………………
………………………………………………………………
………………………………………………………………
………………………………………………………………
………………………………………………………………
………………………………………………………………
………………………………………………………………
………………………………………………………………

Unit 8

accessible *adj* easy to understand, find or reach

atom *n* the smallest unit that an element can be divided into

attachment *n* a computer file which is sent together with an email message

automatically *adv* If a machine or device does something automatically, it does it independently, without human control

back up *pv* to make an extra copy of computer information, e.g. your work

bookmark *n* an address on the internet that you record so that you can quickly find something again

cell *n* the smallest living part of an animal or a plant

claim *v* to say that something is true

concept *n* an idea or principle

conservation *n* the protection of nature

crucial *adj* extremely important or necessary

desktop *n* a computer that is small enough to fit on a desk

extensive *adj* large in amount or size

hard drive *n* the part inside a computer that is not removed and stores very large amounts of information

identify *v* to recognise a problem, need, fact, etc. and to show that it exists

(be/get) inspired *adj* having ideas from someone or something

investigate *v* to try to get all the facts about something

log in/on *pv* to connect a computer to a computer system by typing your name, so that you can start work

log off/out *pv* to stop a computer being connected to a computer system, usually when you want to stop working

monitor *n* a screen that shows information or pictures, usually connected to a computer

necessity *n* something that you need

pedal *v* to push the pedals of a bicycle round with your feet

percentage *n* an amount of something, expressed as a number out of 100

play a trick (on) *exp* to deceive or cheat someone as a joke

reveal *v* to tell or show someone a piece of (secret) information

solve an equation *exp* to find an answer to a mathematical problem

substance *n* a solid, gas or liquid

survive *v* to continue to live or exist, especially after almost dying or being destroyed

technical *adj* relating to the knowledge, machines, or methods used in science and industry

vast *adj* very big

vital *adj* necessary

My words

ANSWER KEY

Unit 1

LISTENING

Part 3

3 1 Emily's family always have a party on New Year's Eve. It's well organised.
   2 They went to a restaurant this year. Everything went well.
   3 Nobody disagreed.

> **Recording script**
>
> On New Year's Eve my family always get together and last year my uncle and his family came over from New Zealand. My mum always plans a party way in advance – she likes cooking and she's really good at organising all the games and everything. Everyone leaves it to her now as she's best at it but my uncle was ahead of her this time and he suggested we should all go out to eat. <u>We'd never thought of doing that, well, just because we never have, but it was fun and everything went smoothly.</u> Everyone agreed though that we really like our traditions, so we'll celebrate at home again next year.

4 E is the correct answer: there was a change of plan (*we'd never thought of doing that*) and it was successful (*it was fun and everything went smoothly*). This tests both understanding of the whole recording (that they changed their plan) and also a detail (it was successful).
   A There is nothing to suggest that it was less well organised than usual.
   B Going out to eat was a change but it wasn't an unexpected event as it was planned in advance.
   C There is nothing to say it lasted longer than usual.
   D There was no difference of opinion (everyone agreed)
   F There is nothing to suggest that the day started off badly.

Exam task

Speaker 1 D
Speaker 2 B
Speaker 3 C

> **Recording script**
>
> *You will hear three people talking about a family celebration. Choose from the list A–F what each speaker says about the celebration.*
>
> *Speaker 1*
>
> My granddad's birthday is on Midsummer Day and the whole family meet up and have a picnic. When my cousins and I were small we loved it, but now we've all got things we do, like I'm in a football team and my cousin has a job in a café. So we suggested we had the party at home instead this year, <u>but that didn't go down well.</u> My parents were OK with it but my aunties said it would upset granddad and all the plans were already made, so I had to miss my football match and the team lost – probably not because of me but you never know.
>
> *Speaker 2*
>
> My cousins live in the city and visit us twice a year. There's never any discussion about what we'll do when they arrive. We pile the cars up with loads of stuff and head down to the beach where we have a huge barbecue. Then everyone does what they want – sit and read or play games or swim or whatever. It's usually a really quiet place but <u>the weird thing was that this time there was someone making a film on the beach and they asked us to be in the background.</u> We didn't mind because we just carried on with what we were doing anyway.
>
> *Speaker 3*
>
> The first of May is a holiday and my family always have a big meal together at home. Usually the weather is nice and we eat outside. We always play the same games and eat the same food and everybody knows what to expect. <u>Usually my grandparents and the others go home when it gets dark but this year was different</u> because my uncle has a new job in Brazil and he and my auntie and cousins are going to live there for three years. <u>When it got dark, nobody moved and we carried on chatting until midnight</u> because we all knew that they wouldn't be here next year.

READING AND USE OF ENGLISH

Part 1

1 1 A at least   B at once   C at last   D at all
   2 A expects   B demands   C depends   D believes

2 1 It is the shortest / longest day.
   2 that the days will start to get longer and lighter

Exam task

1 B   2 D   3 B   4 D   5 C   6 A   7 B   8 A

SPEAKING

Part 1

1.
   1. every Wednesday after school, favourite time
   2. relax first and watch TV
   3. (Saturdays) friends in city centre, shopping, chatting; (Sunday mornings) grandmother
   4. (Saturday) bus to town with friends as usual, probably new cinema in shopping mall; (Sunday) practise guitar for concert on Tuesday

> **Recording script**
>
> Examiner: Hello, George. I'm going to ask you some questions about yourself. Do you do any activities after school?
>
> George: Yes, I do. I'm learning to dive, so I have a lesson every Wednesday after school in the pool. That's my favourite time in the whole week.
>
> Examiner: When do you do your homework?
>
> George: When I get home from school, I watch TV. I like to relax for an hour, so I prefer to do my homework after dinner.
>
> Examiner: Francesca, what do you usually do at the weekend?
>
> Francesca: I usually meet my friends in the city centre on Saturdays and we spend all afternoon shopping and chatting. On Sunday mornings I go to see my grandmother.
>
> Examiner: What are you going to do next weekend?
>
> Francesca: On Saturday I'm going to get the bus to town with my friends as usual and we'll probably go to the cinema. But on Sunday I'll be practising my guitar most of the day as I'm playing in a concert next Tuesday. I know I need to practise a lot before that!

2.
   1. 'm learning
   2. get; watch
   3. 'm going to get
   4. 'll probably go
   5. 'll be practising
   6. 'm playing

Grammar – Present and future tenses

3.
   1. present continuous (*'m learning*)
   2. present simple (*get home, watch TV*)
   3. *going* to (intention); *will* (uncertain future plan)
   4. future continuous as it's over a period of time
   5. present continuous (definite plan)

4. 'A' is correct in each case as they are all state verbs which cannot be used in continuous tenses.

5.
   1. 're meeting
   2. want
   3. normally spend
   4. 're going
   5. think
   6. get
   7. 'm going
   8. go
   9. 'm writing; 'm going to miss
   10. 're coming

Part 2

6. energetic, concentrate, countryside, exercise, indoors, outdoors, a quiet spot, fresh air

7. Photo 1 they're in the fresh air, having fun together, spend less money
   Photo 2 getting more exercise, more energetic

8.

> **Recording script**
>
> In both of the photographs the people are exercising but I think the people in the first photograph are probably much happier than the people in the second one. They're riding their bikes in the countryside, whereas the people in the second photo are indoors on the running machines in the gym, which isn't as enjoyable as <u>being in the fresh air</u>. Also, in the gym they are doing things separately instead of <u>having fun together</u>. On the other hand, they are probably <u>getting more exercise</u> as they are being <u>more energetic</u> than the people in the first photograph. In the first photograph there is a group of friends or maybe cousins even and they're excited about going somewhere together. They're probably chatting as well. <u>They'll spend less money</u> than going to the gym as cycling is free.

9.
   1. The people in the first photo are probably much happier than the people in the second photo.
   2. They will spend less money than going to the gym.
   3. The people in the second photo are indoors, which isn't as enjoyable as being in the fresh air.
   4. They are probably getting more exercise.
   5. They are being more energetic than the people in the first photograph.

READING AND USE OF ENGLISH

Part 5

2.
   1. Sierra's brother is going on a trip and has asked her to go too. She is very excited.

2 Amy feels annoyed that Sierra is going on another trip when she doesn't go anywhere.
3 The trip they are all going on.

Exam task

1 B 2 A 3 D 4 B

Vocabulary – Matching expressions with similar meanings

3   1 keen to get his approval
    2 (He) really thought he was better than the rest of them
    3 very unsure and worried
    4 relaxed, glad that it wasn't him who had been chosen
    5 rather annoyed
    6 suddenly made up his mind
    7 tackle

WRITING

Part 1: Essay

4 1 F (You have no choice. There is one essay task and you have to do it. It's compulsory.)
   2 F (You have to write between 140 and 190 words. 190 is the maximum.)
   3 T (It gives you the topic.)
   4 T (Family and friends)
   5 T (Yes, you are asked to give a general opinion, although you can give examples from your own life and experience as well.)
   6 T (Yes, it should be a fresh idea.)

6

Which is more important to teenagers?	Essay A	Essay B
Main points 1 time	*friends*	*friends*
2 support	*family*	*both*
3 ?	*teenagers get on better with friends*	*family is there throughout your life, friends change*
Conclusion	*friends*	*family*

7   Essay A: <u>In addition</u>, they play sport   <u>Yet</u> all teenagers still rely heavily   <u>In general</u>, though, I would say   <u>Therefore</u>, I personally think
    Essay B: <u>overall</u> I spend slightly more time   <u>As for</u> support   <u>Yet</u> my best friend also helps me   <u>In contrast</u>, some of the friends you make   <u>For that reason</u>, I think that

    1 in general   2 As for   3 In fact   4 For that reason
    5 Yet   6 In contrast

Exam task
Model answer

> Older people can certainly tell us a lot about the past and how the world has changed during their lifetimes. My great aunt is 97; she has memories of a time when there were few opportunities for girls, and has lived through wars and many political crises that I have only read about in history books.
>
> However, many people also say that older people are out of touch with the modern world of technology. I really don't think it's possible to generalise about this. For example, my own grandparents are still at work and they use computers every day. They send me text messages, and my grandmother has a Facebook page which she uses to catch up with friends and family.
>
> In addition, I would like to say that I have learnt a huge amount about people and feelings from my grandparents. They have a lot of experience and they are very wise. If I have a problem, I talk to them about it, and the advice they give me is usually good.
>
> Therefore, I would like to say that I agree very strongly that we can learn a huge amount from grandparents and older people.

Unit 2

READING AND USE OF ENGLISH

Part 6

2 The title tells you he tried to get to the North Pole but he didn't succeed.

3 1 180 km
   2 a guide called Doug
   3 windy and cold
   4 gaps in the ice were too wide for them to cross

4 1 B 2 A 3 D 4 C 5 F 6 E

5 1 *there* in A refers to the North Pole / his destination
   2 *them* in B refers to the few people who had skied to the North Pole
   3 *they* in C refers to temperatures
   4 *him* and *his* in D refer to Doug
   5 *that* in E refers to gaps in the ice
   6 *these* in F refers to cracks

Exam task

1 E 2 A 3 B 4 D

6 A Of course, at some point I realised that I'd got some of <u>those details</u> muddled.
   B <u>They knew they could be killed</u> at any moment through their lack of knowledge or poor judgement.
   C doesn't fit anywhere (*they* were not the only ones and *that* don't fit anywhere)

D <u>That last attempt</u> ended in disaster, for the only thing I achieved was broken bones.

E <u>Most of it</u> went over my head, <u>but the main theme</u> stayed with me.

Grammar – Past tenses

7   1 attempted   2 had reached   3 had travelled   4 went
   5 had been   6 were   7 hadn't / had not seen   8 flew

READING AND USE OF ENGLISH

Part 2

Grammar – Tenses and prepositions

1   1 bought   2 until   3 looked; was happening   4 during
   5 've been trying; haven't finished   6 was coming; saw
   7 at   8 'd forgotten   9 for   10 had disappeared

2   Prepositions: **0, 3, 4, 5,**
    Parts of a verb: **1, 2, 6, 8**
    (7 is a pronoun)

Exam task

1 taken   2 was   3 across   4 At   5 until   6 had   7 none
8 have

Part 3

Vocabulary – Word building (1)

3   *-able:* bearable, considerable, desirable, fashionable, forgettable, predictable, reliable, remarkable, suitable
    -al: accidental, central, controversial, cultural, logical, natural, universal
    -ous: adventurous, furious, mysterious

4   nouns and verbs ending in *-y* usually change the *-y* to an *-i* (*reliable, furious, mysterious*)
    nouns and verbs ending in *-e* usually drop the *-e* (*desirable, central, cultural, natural, universal*)

Exam task

1 adventurous   2 exciting   3 cultural   4 choice   5 locations
6 photographer   7 natural   8 unforgettable

SPEAKING

Part 3

4   A   I agree with you.   That's what I think too.   I think you're right.
    D   I don't think that's a good idea.   I think it would be better to ...   I disagree.

LISTENING

Part 1

2   Picture C (Venice)   bridges over the canals, pedestrian side streets, beautiful buildings, museums, flooding

> **Recording script**
>
> Yeah, well, I've lived here all my life, and I think that makes me really lucky! There's water all around you and bridges over the canals and lots of little pedestrian side streets. And then there are lots of beautiful buildings, palaces and churches – some of them are museums now. It's very flat everywhere though, so we get flooding ...

3   C

> **Recording script**
>
> Well, it's my hometown and I love it! People eat out quite a lot here and you'll find everything from Brazilian food to Spanish tapas. But if I go out with my family we usually eat Italian, pasta and pizza. <u>What I find absolute magic about the city, though, is the street celebrations</u> – they take place all year. In winter, when the snow falls and the days get shorter, we have the Lights Festival in the main square, which is really fantastic. And then of course there's the underground city, which is basically a huge shopping mall. I often go there with my sister – she just adores it, but I find it a bit too big!

4   A is wrong because the shopping mall is what the girl's sister likes; she thinks it's too big.
    B is wrong because the girl simply says she eats out, not that she particularly likes it.

Exam task

1 A   2 C   3 B   4 C

> **Recording script**
>
> *You will hear people talking in four different situations. For questions 1–4, choose the best answer, A, B or C.*
>
> *Question One. You hear a boy talking to his aunt about his new school.*
>
> Woman: So Peter, are you happy at your new secondary school?
>
> Peter: Yeah, very. I've made lots of new friends. <u>It's good because we work well together in class, too, everyone does, there's no messing about ... although we are occasionally the students that get told off for chatting too much!</u>
>
> Woman: Right ...
>
> Peter: ... and it's great learning a language. I'm doing Chinese this year. We've got a lovely teacher, who's really enthusiastic about her subject.

Woman: Sounds good.

Peter: And it's a modern building, with a sports field and a cafeteria. There's a big courtyard too, where you can sit outside and relax between lessons. There was nowhere like that at my last school …

Question Two. You hear two teenagers talking about a film they have just seen.

Girl: So, what did you think then?

Boy: Great, really exciting … I loved the car chases and all that stuff where he was leaping over the roofs. Much better than too much talking …

Girl: But the characters were really good. What they said was quite funny at times. <u>You like fast-moving films then, do you, with a bit of adventure?</u>

Boy: <u>Yeah, doesn't everyone?</u>

Girl: <u>Well, not everyone. I do though.</u> That and some nice scenery to look at – loved the mountains in this one.

Boy: Oh, didn't notice. Liked the film though.

Question Three. You hear a girl talking about a school trip she has been on.

Girl: Yeah, well, we went on a cool trip last week to a modern art gallery. It was in a fantastic building with amazing architecture. It used to be an old factory, and there was just, like, so much space everywhere. There was a sort of library with lots of books and film clips, and it was just so comfortable, with all these big cushions you could sit on. <u>I found out a lot about the background of the person who designed the stuff in the special exhibition on textiles.</u> They were beautiful to look at … really rich colours. I'd love to know what inspired the shapes and patterns on them.

Question Four. You hear two teenagers talking about a friend.

Boy: Hi Lauren, have you seen Mike recently?

Lauren: Yeah, his leg's still in plaster. Such a shame he broke it just before the big match. <u>He's in good spirits though, not being miserable, even though he missed his big chance. I think that's fantastic.</u> It was such a shame he couldn't take part in the final though.

Boy: I know. He's one of their regular players, so I bet the football team missed him. I'm pleased he's reacted OK.

Lauren: Yeah … he'll be able to play again in a few months. That must be encouraging for his team-mates.

Boy: I suppose so. Let's hope they get some goals tomorrow.

Lauren: Right, we can always hope …

WRITING

1   The order is: **1** E   **2** B   **3** D   **4** A   **5** C

Grammar – Past tenses

3   1   looking (the participle belongs with I *was* and describes a continuous action over a period of time)
    2   knew (the verb *know* is not used in the continuous form)
    3   had (past perfect because you are thinking of a period of previous time, before this story starts)
    4   had built (as 3)
    5   heard
    6   realised (the verb *realise* is not used in the continuous form)
    7   was
    8   called
    9   've (present perfect for a very recent action in the past; the plate is probably still in her hand)
   10   rushed
   11   was going (continuous action over a period of time)
   12   disappeared
   13   didn't
   14   got out (one action)
   15   shone (one action)
   16   'd
   17   had

4 Paragraph 1 ends after *centuries ago*, and sets the scene for the story.
Paragraph 2 ends after *disappeared down into a deep hole* and describes the main events of the story.
Paragraph 3 describes what happened to the writer and what he found.

Vocabulary – Adverbs and adjectives

6 1 a worrying   2 a courageous   3 an intriguing   4 a strong
5 a successful   6 aggressive   7 a brilliant   8 a detailed

7 1 calmly   2 positively   3 decisively   4 rapidly
5 efficiently   6 patiently   7 closely   8 regularly

Grammar – Adverb formation

8 1 bitter   2 clumsy   3 happy   4 hopeful   5 miserable
6 positive   7 polite   8 rapid   9 rare   10 simple

1 Adjectives ending in -*y* change their last letter to -*i* before adding -*ly*.
2 Adjectives ending in a consonant and -*le* lose the last letter before adding -*y*.
3 Adjectives ending in -*e* keep the -*e* and add -*ly*.
4 Adjectives ending in -*l* keep the -*l* and add -*ly*.

Exam task

Model answer A

> Max heard someone calling his name excitedly, and turned to see who it was. It was his friend Peter, who rushed over saying that he'd won a prize, a trip to America. 'And there are four tickets,' he said. 'My Mum and Dad are going. Do you want to come with us?'
>
> Max didn't hesitate to say yes. And that was how he found himself on a flight to Florida. At the airport they picked up a hire car and Peter's dad drove them to the hotel. Max and Peter ran rapidly to the swimming pool where they spent a couple of hours swimming and diving.
>
> Then they headed off to the theme park, where they ate hamburgers and tried all the rides, including one very scary rollercoaster, which made them both scream when it reached full speed. And then, right at the highest point, it suddenly stopped. All the electricity had gone off. It was very hot sitting in the sun, but there was nothing they could do except wait patiently until a successful rescue attempt was made.
>
> Fortunately, nothing else went wrong during the rest of the holiday!

Model answer B

> I was amazed when I saw who was sitting in the seat opposite mine in the train. I couldn't believe it was him at first. Then, when he looked up and smiled warmly at me, I knew I was right. What was the most famous football player in the world doing on this train, sitting calmly, reading a football magazine?
>
> I thought I'd ask him. 'Excuse me, David. Why are you travelling by train?'
>
> 'Well,' he said, 'I'm supposed to set a good example to everyone, and not throw my money around, because I do a lot of charity work with young people. And actually I quite like travelling by train. If anyone talks to me, they're usually very polite, like you are. And I like chatting to people.'
>
> That was the best news I had heard in a long time. I asked my hero lots of questions about his work, his family, and when he first discovered he had a talent for football. He answered them all patiently, and before we arrived in London he gave me a signed photo of himself as a souvenir.

Unit 3

LISTENING

Part 4

Person	What (s)he does
actor	acts, performs, plays a part/role
stuntman/woman	does action shots
set decorator	arranges the scenery
director	tells the actors what to do
cameraman/woman	films a scene, takes a shot of something
producer	raises money to make the film
costume designer	designs/fits costumes
sound technician	checks quality of voice recording
make-up artist	does someone's face/hair

2 Picture A   A cameraman is filming a scene on set. There are young actors who are getting ready to film a scene. The woman on the left is the director. She is telling the actors what to do.
Picture B   A make-up artist is doing someone's face and hair.
Picture C   A costume designer is about to fit a costume.
Picture D   A stuntman is doing an action shot in a film.

3 1 You will hear part of an interview with a young actor called Tania West.
2 In what way is Tania like Angie, the character she plays in the film?
   A She doesn't get on well with other people.
   B She doesn't try to impress other people.
   C She doesn't always behave as other people expect.
3 What did Tania find difficult about being on set?
   A working with older actors
   B learning her lines
   C having little time to relax
4 What does Tanya say about her acting schedule?
   A She often filmed at night.
   B She had little trouble getting up early.
   C She missed having regular meals.

4 Suggested answers

a problem she has had

her reactions to her own acting

her own personality

her daily routine

Exam task

1 B   2 C   3 C   4 B

Recording script

You will hear part of an interview with a young actor called Tania West. For questions 1–4, choose the best answer A, B or C.

Interviewer: So, Tania, welcome to the studio.

Tania: Thank you, it's great to be here.

Interviewer: Tania, you've just finished your first film, and been to the opening night – and you're still only 17! What was it like seeing yourself on screen?

Tania: Well, it was kind of weird at first. It's like looking at a giant version of yourself. Before I went to the opening, I thought it might be scary, but it wasn't in the end. I just felt like I was watching my twin! <u>Somehow it just wasn't me up there</u>, yet I could remember how many times I'd had to do the scene, how much of me had gone into it. I certainly wasn't bored watching the film, even though I knew it so well. Everything suddenly came to life …

Interviewer: And were there any similarities between you and Angie, the girl you played on screen?

Tania: Yeah, well it would be nice to think so! <u>She's a bit of a rebel, and I'm a lot like that. I often don't follow normal rules.</u> She doesn't really care what people think about her, though, whereas I do. But because she's very confident, people find it easy to relate to her. I did anyway. I found myself just walking round the studio, pretending to be Angie. That's how I really got into the role. I missed her when we finished shooting!

Interviewer: What was the atmosphere like when you were on set? Did you have any problems?

Tania: Actually, I found it quite stressful. <u>We were on a tight schedule, and there was never any time just to chill out.</u> You were always learning your lines, but fortunately I found that easy because I've got a good memory and the older actors helped me. You form a close bond with other actors, they kind of become like your family really. They were a big part of my life for several months.

Interviewer: And how did you find the daily schedule at the studio? Did you get into a routine?

Tania: We had to be on set, have our make-up done and everything by 7.30, so that meant getting up very early. <u>Fortunately, my family lives quite close to the studio and it didn't bother me.</u> All the actors had breakfast together, and then we shot some scenes, maybe three or four each morning. Then everyone ate lunch and then we shot more scenes in the afternoon. Then on a few occasions we did night-shoots too, and that didn't finish till about two a.m.

Interviewer: But you enjoyed it?

Tania: Oh yes!

WRITING
Part 2

2 The photos are of: Indiana Jones, James Bond, Batman, Lara Croft.

3 1 You can write about **any** type of film, provided it features an impressive hero/heroine. The word *hero* could be used for a man or a woman.

2 The question asks you whether you would *recommend* the film, so it's possible to write a negative review if you think that the storyline or other actors are not good. But the hero you write about must be impressive, and it's much easier to write about a film you enjoyed!

4 1 Yes, especially the hero and the villain.

2 Yes, because it says the film makes you think and that it's interesting.

3 Present tense. The alternative is the past tense. Either is acceptable, but you must be consistent about your use of tenses. Write the whole review either in the present tense OR in the past tense(s), but don't use a mixture of the two.

4 The candidate gives the work a title so the reader knows immediately which film is being talked about.

5 The sentence which sums up the candidate's view of the film is: *In my opinion, this film is outstanding*.

5 *film:* dark N; difficult N; disturbing N; amazing action scenes P; outstanding P; thrilling P

Batman: action hero P; symbol of justice P; brave P; determined P

Joker: psychopathic N; scary N

6 Para 1 introduction – describe the film, makes you *think* + amazing action scenes

Para 2 content of film – describe Batman and his *character* and how he fights organised *crime* and The *Joker*

Para 3 conclusion – sum up film and *recommend* it (explain why)

7

This is a classic in the Batman series. It is a dark, difficult and at times rather disturbing film, <u>which</u> really makes you think. <u>As</u> you sit in the audience, you wonder what would happen if a hero like Batman really came along and decided to deal with organised crime in our big cities, <u>yet</u> you are <u>also</u> entertained <u>because</u> the film has a lot of amazing action scenes.

In *The Dark Knight*, Batman is an action hero, <u>but more importantly</u> he is <u>also</u> a symbol of justice. He is a brave and determined character <u>who</u> teams up with the forces of law and order in the city of Gotham, ready to take on all the crime lords. <u>As a result</u>, he has to face a psychopathic and very scary villain called The Joker.

<u>In my opinion</u>, this film is outstanding. It is <u>not only</u> thrilling <u>but</u> it <u>also</u> makes you feel as if you are experiencing what is going on. <u>When</u> I saw it, everyone in the audience was totally involved in it, <u>so</u> I'd say it's a film you really must see.

Exam task

Model answers

> **The best thriller ever:** *Bullitt*
>
> I saw this old film again recently on DVD and it's still fantastic. It stars Robert Vaughan as an ambitious politician who wants to fight organised crime and Steve McQueen as Bullitt, one of the detectives whose job is to protect him. The film has a very complicated plot. Bullitt has to be very clever to catch the criminals and stop the politician from being murdered.
>
> The film is still famous after many years because it has some amazing action scenes, with Bullitt driving a green Ford Mustang car. The most famous scene is a car chase, with two bad guys chasing Bullitt up the hills in San Francisco. They go everywhere, including up and down the steps that San Francisco is famous for. It's so exciting it takes your breath away! The other great chase is at the airport, on the runways. It's amazing.
>
> I would definitely recommend this film. In my opinion, it is outstanding. It makes you feel as if you are experiencing what is going on. You will enjoy it because the action scenes keep you on the edge of your seat. (186 words)

> **Romantic Comedy:** *One Day*
>
> This is a very interesting story because of the way it is told. The two main characters, Dexter and Emma, meet at university and become best friends. They both get romantically involved with other people, and there are lots of amusing moments. The film explains how their lives turn out by showing you what happens over the years on just one day each year.
>
> There are big highs and lows in this film. At first you think Dexter and Emma will never get together, but in the end they do, and for a while they are incredibly happy. But then the film changes; it all ends in tragedy, and Dexter is nearly destroyed as a person, until his father is able to rescue him and show him how to get on with his life and make a new start.
>
> I really like it; the ending is very unusual for a romantic comedy, which I think is one of the best things about the film. I'd recommend anyone who enjoys romantic comedies to see this film. (182 words)

READING AND USE OF ENGLISH

Part 7

1 The instruments are (left to right): guitar, flute, drums, clarinet, violin, saxophone, keyboard, cello, piano

2 1 ✓ (contains songs = *have lyrics*, whose words will appeal to a certain age group = *which focus on the kinds of emotions that teenagers really relate to*)

  2 ✗ (the text says the opposite – *there's no way you could describe it as depressing*)

  3 ✗ (*it seems things can only go up for them* so it will probably be more rather than less popular than the last one)

  4 ✗ (the last album *introduced a new sound* which this one develops)

  5 ✓ (likely to extend the success = *expected to further widen the band's appeal*)

  6 ✓ (particular style = *a very unusual voice*, well matched = *they suit him perfectly*)

  7 ✓ (the writer is happy with most of the singing being *done by Kez*)

3 1 The reviews are mainly positive.

Exam task

1 **D** (will set high standards for her second)

2 **B** (some tunes are difficult to distinguish from each other)

3 **A** (focusing on topics other artists seem to prefer not to sing about)

4 **C** (her teen audience is sure to mature and grow along with her)

5 **D** (there are several songs that could easily have been left out, resulting in a better album overall)

6 A (after a two-year wait, in spite of pressure from fans and their record company)
7 B (the best song is not the most well known)
8 C (While some bands … the Lantanas are by contrast a rare find)

Grammar – Linking words

4 A Breeze has released *Pedal Street* after a two-year wait, <u>in spite of</u> pressure from fans and their record company to do so earlier.

  B <u>However</u>, she then shows just what the band is about with the roaring, angry growl that follows. <u>Although</u> some tunes are difficult to distinguish from each other in the sense that Tarrant's voice doesn't vary from song to song, the album will soon be permanently fixed on your playlist.

  C <u>While</u> some bands incorporate good beats but have cliché lyrics that make you feel slightly sick, or sing songs with meaningful words, yet make a dreadful sound, the Lantanas are by contrast a rare find.

  D <u>Despite</u> having a more limited vocal range than her sister who is also a singer, April proves that she does have a big talent for writing.

  It is an excellent combination of easy listening <u>even though</u> there are several songs that could have easily been left out, resulting in a better album overall,.

1 Despite / In spite of   **2** However,   **3** even though / although
4 Even though / Although   **5** However,   **6** Despite / In spite of

SPEAKING

Part 2

4

> **Recording script**
>
> Examiner: In this part of the test, I'm going to give each of you two pictures. I'd like you to talk about the pictures on your own for about a minute, and also to answer a question about your partner's pictures.
>
> *[to candidate A]* It's your turn first. Here are your pictures. They show people watching different kinds of films. I'd like you to compare the pictures, and say what you think people might enjoy about these films. All right?
>
> Candidate A: Well, in the first picture, a mouse is being chased by a cat and I suppose he'll be caught soon. When I was a child, I used to like programmes like this very much, <u>you know, the sort of films</u> which have drawings not actors. I think children always like them, and adults often enjoy them too.
>
> In my opinion, the film in the second picture is more exciting. It's a thriller and these people are … <u>well, let's say</u> a bank has just been robbed <u>or something like that</u>. That's why the men in the black car are being chased by the police. They'll probably be arrested soon and will be taken to the police station. Most young people like thrillers, especially if there is a lot of action and a nice hero or heroine. People of all ages like them actually.
>
> Examiner: *[to candidate B]* And which of these films would you prefer to see?
>
> Candidate B: OK, I'd prefer to see the second film. I'd definitely enjoy the thriller. I think it's better to see a really exciting film that you can enjoy and get involved in.
>
> Examiner: Thank you. Now, here are your photographs. They show people playing music in different situations. I'd like you to compare the photographs, and say why you think music is important to these different groups of people.
>
> Candidate B: Well the first photo shows some kids dancing to music in the street. It's a special kind of street dance <u>I don't know the name of</u>. The music is being played on a sound system with huge speakers. Most of the people are smiling and they look happy. I guess this is just their way of escaping and having fun. It's all part of their image, too, part of their identity. And then when you look at the other picture, the children in the photo of the school orchestra, they look very … <u>well … er … um … I'd say</u> definitely not relaxed. They look like this is something they have to do. I guess some of them were persuaded to do it by their parents or a teacher. I think they might be rehearsing for a concert and I expect the concert will be attended by the parents. I suppose it will prove to them that their children are very talented, so maybe it's a big challenge for them … for the children, I mean …
>
> Examiner: Thank you. *[to candidate A]* And which of the activities would you prefer to do?
>
> Candidate A: Mm … that's a difficult choice because I'd sooner not do them at all.

> Examiner: Why not?
>
> Candidate A: I can't dance very well, and I'm not the slightest bit musical! But perhaps if I had to do one of them, I'd rather play in the orchestra than do dancing in the street ...
>
> Examiner: Thank you.

5 1 ... you know, the *sort of* films which have *drawings*, not actors
   2 ... these people are ... well, *let's say* a bank has just been robbed or *something like that*
   3 It's a *special kind of* street dance I don't know the *name of* ...
   4 ... the children in the photo of the school orchestra, they look very ... well ... er ... um ... I'd say definitely not relaxed.

6 cartoons, robbers, breakdance, serious / stressed

7

> **Recording script**
>
> Examiner: And which of these films would you prefer to see?
>
> Candidate B: OK, <u>I'd prefer to</u> see the second film. <u>I'd definitely</u> enjoy the thriller. <u>I think it's better to</u> see a really exciting film that you can enjoy and get involved in.
>
> Examiner: Thank you.
>
> Examiner: And which of the activities would you prefer to do?
>
> Candidate A: Mm ... that's a difficult choice because <u>I'd sooner</u> not do them at all.
>
> Examiner: Why not?
>
> Candidate A: I can't dance very well, and I'm not the slightest bit musical! But perhaps if I had to do one of them, <u>I'd rather</u> play in the orchestra <u>than</u> do dancing in the street ...
>
> Examiner: Thank you.

READING AND USE OF ENGLISH
Part 4

Grammar – The passive

1 Candidate A
   1 ... a mouse *is being chased* by a cat and I suppose *he'll be caught* soon.
   2 ... a bank *has just been robbed* or something like that. That's why the men in the black car *are being chased* by the police. *They'll probably be arrested* soon and *will be taken* to the police station.
   Candidate B
   3 The music *is being played* on a sound system with huge speakers.
   4 I guess some of them *were persuaded* to do it by their parents or teacher.
   5 ... I expect the concert *will be attended* by the parents.

2

tenses	verb form	past participle
present simple	are	felt
present continuous	is / are being	chased / played
future simple	will be	caught / arrested / taken / attended / fixed
past simple	was / were	persuaded / recorded
present perfect	has been	robbed / allowed / looked forward to
past perfect	had been	told
with modals	could have been	left out
	would be	improved

3 (Passives from reading text and questions are in italics in the table.)
   Fans *had been told* to expect something special (A)
   emotions that *are felt* by everybody (A)
   which *was recorded* over two years (B)
   the album *will soon be permanently fixed* on your playlist (B)
   Lena *has been allowed* to sing all types of song here (C)
   could easily have been left out (D)
   would be improved (Q5)
   has been looked forward to for some time (Q6)

4 1 This castle *was built* in the twelfth century.
   2 I was *given* a leaflet which contained some interesting information.
   3 The band *was* first established in 1992.
   4 These days music *is made* by computers.
   5 My best friend *is* called Ann-Marie.
   6 The concert *was* supposed to start at 7.00, but the guitarist arrived late.
   7 My house *is* located in a beautiful area.
   8 The business studies course *was* cancelled at the last minute.
   9 *Is* lunch *included* / Will lunch *be included* in the price of the school trip?
   10 My family stay in a house that *is* situated a few miles from the beach.

5 1 A is correct. B is in the wrong tense. C is grammatically correct but doesn't use the prompt word BEEN.

2 B is correct. A *disappointed* is wrong; a noun is needed. C has too many words and doesn't use the prompt word WAS.
3 C is correct. A is in the wrong tense. B is missing the verb *be*.
4 A is correct. B is missing the verb *is*. C has the wrong preposition (*to*).
5 C is correct. A and B both include *to* and B also omits 'd.

Exam task

1 was built by
2 was knocked over by
3 has been played more
4 will have been handed in
5 will be worn by
6 will be given less

Unit 4

READING AND USE OF ENGLISH

Part 5

1 The top five sports in the world are football, cricket, hockey, tennis and volleyball.
2 do athletics   play badminton   play cricket   go cycling   play football   do gymnastics   play hockey   go ice skating   do martial arts   go snowboarding   go surfing   play tennis   play volleyball   go windsurfing   do yoga
4 *Football*: defender, goalkeeper, net, opponent, penalty, pitch, referee, tackle
   Tennis: court, net, opponent, point, serve, umpire
   lap, *race* and *track* are used for athletics (or field and track) and motor racing
5 **A** – Paragraph 3
   B – Paragraph 4
   C – Paragraph 2
   D – Paragraph 1

Exam task

1 D   2 C   3 A   4 B

LISTENING

Part 2

1 Sentence 4 needs an adjective.
2 1 brother, friend, photographer, sister, uncle
   2 friend, photographer, post, rock, tree
   3 brakes, route, tyres, weather
   4 comfortable, stylish, tight, warm
3 1 uncle   2 photographer   3 tyres   4 tight

Recording script

When I was about 13, my dad bought my brothers a mountain bike each because all their friends had one, but, because we were girls, my sister and I were given ordinary bikes that were no good for racing. I really wanted to join my brothers, so in the end <u>my uncle got one for me</u> and my sister.

My sister never really got into it, but I spent all my time out on my bike and started to enter competitions. I just won the Regional Championship and I beat all the boys. It was a difficult course, with lots of rocks and stony bits, and at one point I thought I wasn't going to win. I was ahead and then I had to slow down because <u>a photographer jumped out from behind a tree</u>.

I'm very careful with my preparation for races. I look at the route and make sure everything's working on the bike. The brakes need to be in perfect condition especially if the weather's wet. Then, <u>just before I set off, I take a look at the tyres</u>. If there's any problem with them, then I'll be in trouble. Also, it's really important to wear the right clothes. They shouldn't get in the way or slow you down so <u>they need to be tight</u>. They might feel a bit uncomfortable when you first put them on but you soon get used to it. I'm not bothered about looking fashionable or stylish – I just want to win.

Exam task

1 second   2 stretch   3 audience   4 S/stars on ice   5 music
6 swimming

Recording script

You will hear part of a talk by a young skater called Karl Milton. For questions 1–6, complete the sentences with a word or short phrase.

I'm training very hard at the moment because I'm hoping to be picked for the Olympic ice-skating team. I should have been in the team four years ago – well, that's what my coach said. But I was left out, so I'm determined to be selected this time. I competed in a national championship last week and so did my brother – he skates too. Jack Graham was defending the title – you might have seen him on TV afterwards – and he must have been practising all the time as he was even better than last year and finished

first. But I was <u>second</u>, just behind him, and my brother came third, so we were both pleased. Either of us could have won but you just never know who's going to do best on the day.

To be good enough to win competitions, I need to be really fit. Obviously I practise every day and I spend a lot of my time on the ice doing spins and jumps to get them exactly right. But I skate really badly if I ever forget to stretch. That's really crucial and something all skaters have to do, so I spend about thirty or forty minutes doing that every day before and after I go on the ice. It keeps me flexible as well as free from injury.

I enjoy competitions but I do get nervous, so I never think about the skaters I'm competing against. I just focus on the audience and hope they're enjoying it – then I skate well. If I start thinking about the judges, then I make mistakes.

And something new for me, I'm going to be a judge myself soon. I always loved the TV show *Ice Champions* when I was a child and now I'm going to be one of the judges of *Stars on Ice*, which is for teenagers. I'd say to any contestant wanting to do well, you should build up your confidence so that you put on a really smooth and entertaining show. Each skater has a partner. They can't choose who they skate with and they have to follow a certain routine, but they can decide which music they want to skate to.

I'm hoping one day to have more time for hobbies. I go swimming whenever I can – that was my first love before skating and it helps me with my moves on the ice. I'd love to go horse riding or play tennis, but although they would be good for building up muscles and fitness, I can't fit everything in! And now I need to go and do some training …

Grammar – Modal verbs

4   **1** should   **2** can't   **3** have to   **4** can   **5** should have been   **6** must have been practising   **7** could have won

5   is allowed – **4** (*can*)
    seems certain – **6** (*must have*)
    is advised – **1** (*should*)
    isn't allowed – **2** (*can't*)
    was possible – **7** (*could have*)
    is a rule – **3** (*have to*)
    was expected – **5** (*should have*)

6   **1** don't have to   **2** should   **3** must have been   **4** mustn't   **5** had to   **6** must

READING AND USE OF ENGLISH
Part 2

Grammar – Prepositions following verbs and adjectives

1   **1** on   **2** for   **3** of   **4** with   **5** about   **6** of   **7** about   **8** about   **9** in   **10** to

Exam task

1   **1** the   **2** or   **3** in   **4** on   **5** there   **6** your   **7** such   **8** like

Part 3

Vocabulary – Word building (2)

2   similarity (similar +ity)
    conclusion (conclude de +sion)
    suggestion (suggest +ion)

3   confidence   convenience   curiosity   equality   generosity
    independence   patience   possibility
    appreciation   concentration   connection   decoration
    division   expansion   production   reaction

Exam task

1   **1** popularity   **2** madness   **3** successful   **4** increasingly   **5** variety   **6** introduction   **7** choice   **8** unacceptable

Vocabulary – Food

4   fatty   nutty   salty   spicy   tasty

5   *diet:* balanced, healthy, low-fat, rich, vegetarian
    meat: fried, low-fat, raw, tough, rotten
    fruit: raw, ripe, rotten, seasonal
    pudding: rich, sugary

WRITING
Part 2: Letter and email

2   **1** don't worry too much about   **2** remember that   **3** it should   **4** it'd be better to   **5** I suggest you   **6** Why not   **7** recommend doing   **8** you can

3   **1** T   **2** F (He talks about all three)   **3** F   **4** T   **5** F (He wishes him luck)   **6** T (The style is fairly informal i.e. it's direct, and Pete uses short forms, but the letter doesn't contain lots of slang or idioms; it's grammatically correct.)

5   **1** E   **2** C   **3** A   **4** D   **5** B
    The email reads better with the extra sentences because there is more detail and interest. The writer is adding personal opinion and experience, and improving the way the email flows.

6   **1** informal   **2** friend   **3** will   **4** don't   **5** usually (there will sometimes be a request for information about something e.g. …so please send me some information about what happens in your country.)   **6** both are acceptable   **7** should   **8** less than (it's better to write 170–190)

7   Start: *Hi* and *hello* are more informal, and often used in emails. *Dear* is often used in a letter.

Finish: *All the best, best wishes, Good luck with everything, Love,* Hope that helps are good ways of finishing informal letters and emails. *Yours* and *With kind regards* are found at the end of formal letters and emails.

Exam task

Model answer A

Hi Sarah

Well, I think going to spend two weeks with your German pen friend sounds like a wonderful idea. I wonder why your parents don't want you to go? If it's very expensive to get there, then I can understand why it's a problem. Otherwise, I'm sure you will be very safe staying with a family, you'll learn about everyday life in Germany and you'll certainly come home speaking the language better.

So, what can you do to persuade your parents to let you go? Well, perhaps you could ask your German teacher if she would speak to them about it as I'm sure he or she will think it's a good idea? Or ask your pen friend to ask her parents to write to your parents? That way they will know it will be a good educational experience for you, and that you will be comfortable with the German family. My only other idea is that you ask your pen friend to stay with you first, so your parents will know that she is a nice girl of the same age.

Does that help? Write and let me know, won't you?

Love,

Anya

Model answer B

Hello Sam

It sounds as though you are in a difficult situation. I know you've always loved football, but I know you are also a good drum player, so it's a tough choice. But actually, I wonder if you have to choose?

There will probably be football matches every week, but I'm sure you will only have concerts once or twice a term and you'll know in advance when they are going to be. If that's right, why don't you explain the situation to your football coach, and ask if it's okay if you miss a match occasionally? There are always other players who can take your place, aren't there, so perhaps he will be okay with the idea? If that's no good, then you'll have to make a choice. You know I'd always choose the sport; it keeps you fit, and you make lots of friends in the team. And as you know, I'm not at all musical. But for you, I don't know – maybe just do whichever will make you happier. And if everything else fails, toss a coin!

Good luck with it.

All the best,

Pieter

Unit 5

READING AND USE OF ENGLISH

Part 7

1 1 sympathetic 2 communicative 3 adventurous 4 competitive 5 creative 6 capable

2 A climbing instructor B nurse C (infant) teacher D sculptor

3 Suggested answers

climbing instructor: adventurous, capable, communicative, energetic

nurse: capable, cheerful, communicative, decisive, sympathetic

(infant) teacher: capable, cheerful, communicative, creative, energetic, sympathetic

sculptor: creative, thorough

Exam task

1 D 2 B 3 C 4 A 5 B 6 D 7 B 8 C 9 A 10 D

READING AND USE OF ENGLISH

Part 1

Vocabulary – Phrasal verbs

2 1 come up with 2 put up with 3 come across 4 give up 5 point out 6 look down on 7 look up to 8 stand out

Exam task

1 C 2 A 3 B 4 D 5 B 6 C 7 D 8 A

Part 4

Grammar – Conditionals

3 1 'd spend 2 wouldn't have found out 3 'll have to 4 have to

4 a 2 b 3 c 1 d 4

5 1 unless
   2 in case
   3 providing (that) / provided (that); as / so long as

6 1 unless 2 if 3 in case 4 so long as

Exam task

1 unless we practise 2 provided my sister is 3 in case there is not / isn't 4 would have done some 5 looking forward to finding 6 need to practise (for)

LISTENING

Part 2

2 attend, primary school, secondary school, state, comprehensive, streamed, set, uniform, sports kit, pupils, playing fields, canteen, laboratories, library, swimming pool, homework

ANSWER KEY 115

Recording script

I attended a <u>primary</u> school in the village where I lived. I started when I was four and stayed there until I was 11, when I moved to the secondary school where I am now. Both are state schools, so they're free, and my secondary school is comprehensive, but we're streamed for certain subjects like maths and languages. I'm much better at numbers than words, so I'm in the highest group for <u>maths</u>, but not for languages. I'm in the second set for those, and I study Spanish and German. We all go to school in uniform, and put on special sports kit whenever we're playing sport of any kind. For the girls, it's <u>blue shorts</u> and a white polo shirt. They're very practical.

Moving to secondary school was quite hard for me because it meant catching the <u>school bus</u> instead of walking, and the school is very big – there are over 1,000 pupils. The facilities are good though. There are playing fields at the back where we can do sport, and there's a proper canteen. And there are science laboratories and quite a big library and a swimming pool. My life's very busy now. I get homework every night, and I play in the school orchestra and the hockey team.

3   attended – went to   catching – getting
     highest group – top set   put on – wear

4   **1** primary   **2** maths   **3** blue shorts   **4** school bus

7   Suggested vocabulary: *plane, wing, shelter, pilot, cockpit, control, radio*

8   **1** not far from   **2** building   **3** didn't appear   **4** press
     5 defended   **6** amazed   **7** hard   **8** described   **9** built
     10 came to a close

Exam task

1 airport   **2** rock   **3** maps   **4** button   **5** attack   **6** jets
7 size   **8** servicing   **9** wood   **10** radio

Recording script

You will hear a student called Max talking about his visit to the Aeroseum in Gothenburg, Sweden. For questions 1–10, complete the sentences with a word or short phrase.

Well, I'm going to talk about my visit to the Aeroseum in Gothenburg in Sweden. I went there with my technology class. It was really interesting and we all enjoyed it. We arrived about half past nine in the morning and we were met by our guide, who fortunately spoke very good English!

The museum is located in some underground shelters not far from a former <u>airport</u>, which was used by the military. Building the shelters was a huge project. Work started in the 1940s and then continued in the 1950s. The guide told us that they had to carve out and move tons of <u>rock</u>, which is much harder than digging out earth. And we found out later that no-one knew anything about the existence of the shelters till just over twenty years ago, when work on creating the museum began. That was because they didn't appear on <u>maps</u> and were kept secret, even from people who lived locally.

And when you enter the museum, you realise how much thought went into the design. First, you have to press a <u>button</u> outside the main doors. As each person does this, the number on the counter screen changes, so you can see exactly how many people are inside at any one time – that's a safety thing. Then there is a loud 'beep' and the doors slide open. They weigh about 180 tons and are about a metre thick, so the building would have been well defended against <u>attack</u>!

I was expecting to see some really old planes, so I was amazed that the first thing you see when you go in are some <u>jets</u>, which look as if they could have been built quite recently. I got a very clear impression of what the shelter was like when it was in active use in the 1950s. And the great thing about this museum is that nothing is off limits; you can climb into any of the exhibits. I really enjoyed getting into one of the cockpits. I was expecting the controls to be complex, but the <u>size</u> of it astonished me. It was so small. It must have been really hard for the pilot to cope with.

After that, our guide told us about the photo gallery, which has pictures of the site construction, and photos of the people who lived and worked in the building over the decades. I didn't find that so interesting, but later on we met a man who volunteers in the gallery now and was happy to describe his experiences of flying planes from the airport and <u>servicing</u> them underground. That was fascinating.

Another thing I really liked was watching people hard at work restoring some of the old planes. The amazing thing was that some of them were working on a wing, and the frame was built of <u>wood</u>, just like the models I've been making. Once that had been made, the wing was covered with fabric, using lots of layers to give it strength. I have to say it didn't look very strong to me, and it was very delicate work!

We stopped for refreshments and then spent more time looking at other aircraft displays before making our way through some of the service tunnels, which were used to bring in supplies, and then going to the control room, where we learned all about 'holding patterns' – the way aircraft are held above the airport, circling round until they can land. We then moved into the radio room, where another volunteer told us about his work and our visit came to a close.

I had a great time. We were there for about three hours and I have to say I could happily have stayed for much longer. I learned a lot and it was really hands on – living history; it meant something to me. Now, I've got some photos to show you, so if you just hang on …

SPEAKING

Part 1

3 1 C   2 B   3 D   4 A

WRITING

Part 2: Set text

Exam task

It is not possible to supply model answers to the questions as set texts change frequently. However, examples of set text answers can be found in the Writing Guide.

Unit 6

LISTENING

Part 4

1 A bushes, rocks, sunshine, grass
   B snow and ice, volcano, grey sky, mountains
   C lake, mountains, pine trees, snow and ice
   D grass, sunshine, bushes
2 A Australia   B Iceland   C Canada   D Cameroon
3 Speaker 1 Iceland   Speaker 2 Cameroon   Speaker 3 Canada
   1 volcanoes, island, Arctic, snow and temperatures below zero
   2 rainy season, very large country, semi-desert, game reserves, giraffes, humid, tropical, rainforest
   3 cold weather and snow, summer - extreme heat, –25°C, heated houses, the fall

Recording script

Speaker 1

Yeah, well several of the volcanoes in my country have erupted in recent years, and thrown huge clouds of dust into the sky. This ash is dangerous for aircraft, so there have been times when airports all over Europe have had to close down. It's very dark everywhere when a volcano has just erupted. Normally, though, the weather in my country is mild all year because we're an island. Our summers don't get very hot, and our winters are rarely very cold. But because we're located between the cold air and sea of the Arctic and the warmer air and sea of the more temperate countries, we sometimes get several seasons in a day: sunshine and mild temperatures; windy, cool temperatures and rain; snow and temperatures below zero! Weird eh?!

Speaker 2

The cities in my country are getting hotter, and we get a lot of industrial pollution now. In addition, the ocean is warming, and sea levels are rising. We've always had quite a lot of flooding during the rainy season, and that's getting worse, much more extreme. The whole continent is experiencing climate change.

I live in a very large country, so the climate varies according to where you are. For example, in the far north, there's a semi-desert with mineral deposits and fantastic game reserves with giraffes and things. That contrasts with the land along the coast, which is humid and tropical, and where there's a mixture of rainforest and farmland. And finally, the areas inland are much cooler and wetter than the coast because there is regular rainfall.

Speaker 3

People often associate my country with cold weather and snow, but in fact the climate is very diverse. There are four very distinct seasons. In summer, temperatures can rise to 35°Celsius and higher, and scientists are saying that this extreme heat will increase with global warming. In winter, when most parts of the country have snow, temperatures fall as low as –25°Celsius but we manage to stay warm because we have heated houses, cars and public transportation systems. Some cities have even installed walkways to and from buildings in schools, although mine hasn't got one yet! Spring is generally pleasant and very mild. The fall is often cool, but really bright, with rich orange and red leaves on trees. That's certainly my favourite time of year. OK, so …

4 *Adjectives*: mild, hot, cold, warm, windy, cool, humid, extreme, tropical, wet, bright
Nouns: sunshine, snow, (regular) rain(fall), flooding, heat
Expressions: several seasons in a day, distinct seasons, temperatures below zero, the ocean is warming, sea levels are rising, is experiencing climate change, temperatures fall as low as –25°C, rainy season.

6 Suggested answers

forests disappearing – Brazil
volcanoes erupting – Italy
industrial pollution – the USA, Brazil
rivers drying up – Spain
lack of rain – Saudi Arabia, Spain
flooding – the USA, Bangladesh
hurricanes – Jamaica, the USA
ice melting – Switzerland

Grammar – Countable and uncountable nouns

7 Countable nouns can be singular or plural.
Uncountable nouns cannot be plural and take a singular verb.

8 *Countable*: lake, bushes, mountains, trees, volcanoes, rocks, temperature, season, ocean, hurricane, forests
Uncountable: grass, snow, ice, sky, sunshine, rain, heat, flooding (NB *flood* is countable)

Exam task

1 B 2 C 3 B 4 A 5 B 6 A 7 C

Recording script

You will hear a boy called Tim talking about a school project he has done on the environment. For questions 1–7, choose the best answer (A, B or C).

Teacher: Tim, why did you choose to do your project on 'how to lead a greener life'?

Tim: Well, we'd done a lot about global warming and climate change in our science lessons. It was all a bit complicated really, but I knew something about the big issues. I found it all rather negative and depressing. So, I decided to think small, and see what I could do in my own life, rather than just act completely helpless. And I knew the rest of my family would be interested.

Teacher: Did you find it easy to get information?

Tim: Yeah. I discovered there were lots of people of my age blogging about being green. There was stuff about transport, and ways of getting to school each day. I'd always gone by car – Mum used to drop me off and then drive across town to work. Catching a bus would be better, from the environmental point of view, but we're not on a bus route, so I've gone for riding my bike to school now. Some of my friends live close to the school, so they can walk, but that's not possible for me.

Teacher: OK, and what about being green once you're actually at school?

Tim: Well, I looked up how schools could make better use of resources like paper. I realised that although all school paper was recycled, we used huge quantities, and I thought we should cut down. And then it came to me – it's obvious really – that we should be sending in most of our work electronically, you know, by email attachment. I'm going to recommend it to our school council – the people from each class who give the head teacher suggestions from pupils. I read about something called GOOS paper too, that's paper that's still 'good on one side', and actually most of my friends do that already – use both sides I mean.

Teacher: And what about the school cafeteria?

Tim: We could make that environmentally friendly as well. One school I've read about has 'meatless Mondays'. Apparently, if we eat less meat, we use far less of the world's resources, and animals like cows and sheep pollute the atmosphere with methane gas! It's good to use local produce too, so we don't have to transport it far. That's something our school already does. But we still have machines with bottled milk, water and juice for sale, and I think we should just have jugs of water on the tables instead.

Teacher: Did you think about life at home too?

Tim: Yeah, I think families are high energy consumers, especially now many homes are built with air conditioning. <u>People of my age use huge amounts of power by leaving computer screens and game boxes running 24/7 – they're never turned off! Now that's something we can all do something about!</u> Fortunately, there are improvements like energy-efficient light bulbs though, which most people now have.

Teacher: And what about water? That's a precious resource in every country in the world!

Tim: Absolutely, so we should ask ourselves whether we really need a long hot bath when we get in from playing football! Wouldn't taking a quick shower do? <u>And hands up anyone who leaves the tap on when they brush their teeth. Do you need to do that? Of course you don't. And if you're putting your sports clothes in the washing machine, use a cold setting if you can.</u> Your parents will be happy because you'll use less electricity!

Teacher: Did you think about shopping?

Tim: Yeah, families can do a lot to help the environment and reduce waste when they go to a food store. You don't need a new plastic bag every time you shop. You should take your own bags with you, and buy drinks in a glass bottle if you can, because glass is always recycled. <u>It's better to cut down on food which is packaged</u>, and if you do continue to purchase ready prepared food rather than cooking with fresh ingredients, take the cardboard packets to the recycling bank, don't just chuck them in the dustbin!

Teacher: Thanks, Tim.

SPEAKING

Part 3

2 1 I don't really think that's a good idea. (D)
   2 Absolutely. (A)
   3 We all know we shouldn't drop litter. (C)
   4 We could tell everyone to turn off their computers at the end of the lesson. (S)
   5 I don't think turning the heating down would go down well with students here. (C)
   6 I'm with you on that. (A)
   7 That's not what I think, I'm afraid. (D)
   8 What about getting recycling bins in the canteen? (S)

WRITING

Part 2: Article

1 1, 2, 4, 6

2 (The numbers in brackets refers to the strategies in exercise 1)

What I do to be 'green' at home and at school

We all have to do something to help the environment, don't we? (**1**) I'm only 14 though, so there's no way I personally can do anything about the really big problems, like climate change, is there? (**1**)

However, I can make sure I live my own life in a green way. It is about making little changes which make a big difference. At home that means not taking baths, because they use too much hot water. (**6**) (Don't worry, I still take showers!) (**2**) I turn off the lights and heating in my room when I leave, so I don't waste electricity. (**6**) I'm very green when it comes to transport too, because I walk everywhere.(**6**) When I go out with my family we often take the train rather than the car, especially if we want to go into the city, and also it's quicker and parking is expensive. (**6**)

At school, I help to collect and recycle all the rubbish. That involves collecting everything from the cafeteria. (**6**) Our head teacher has also decided to turn the central heating on a month later than usual. It's OK, I've put my jumper on! (**2**)

So I can honestly say that I'm as green as I can be. Are you? (**1, 4**)

3 The article is in a fairly formal style. Articles will normally be written for a school or college magazine, or for a teenage website, so this is appropriate. They should be lively, catch the reader's attention and give personal opinion and anecdote.

It's effective to start with a question (often a tag) in order to involve the reader. It's possible to end with a statement, e.g. *Once you start thinking in a green way, it's surprising how many ideas you can come up with*, or a suggestion/comment e.g. *Let's all do what we can to save our planet. / I think we should all do what we can to save the planet.*

5 Model answer

My favourite time of year

Don't you just love the summer? Like all young people I adore it, and especially the month of July.

Why do I love July? Most of all (**1**) <u>because</u> school has finished and, although of course we are really, really sad not to be working at our hot, sweaty desks, it (**2**) <u>means</u> going to the beach with my friends, relaxing on the warm sand, swimming and snorkelling. (**3**) <u>When it comes to</u> eating out, we often go and eat at a little restaurant on the beach, (**4**) <u>especially if</u> we want to meet my aunt and cousins. We always spend the evenings there too, when it's warm, the stars are shining and the music is playing, it's absolute magic. Wouldn't anyone love this experience? For me summer (**5**) <u>is about</u> not having any stress or pressure, relaxing and enjoying the sunshine. (**6**) <u>However</u>, we sometimes have to travel miles to visit relatives who I hardly know, so it isn't all about having fun. Fortunately we get on well for the short time we are together!

I can honestly say that I hope my summers will always be like this. What more could anyone ask for?

Exam task

Model answer A

What I love and hate about the weather in my country

Do you enjoy hot summers on the beach and cold snowy winters? Well, don't come and live in Holland!

We hardly ever get hot summers, and I hate that. However, the weather is mild throughout the year, and it's easy to get about, even if the skies are grey and it rains quite a lot! You don't get your car stuck in the snow on the way to school, and it's never so hot that you need air-conditioning. That is something I appreciate, even though I wouldn't say I loved it!

As a result of the mild but damp weather, the Dutch people walk and cycle a lot, always with their umbrella and their macs, because we are cheerful people who like being outside.

We do get some cold frosty mornings in winter, and maybe a little sprinkle of snow, and when that happens, I love it. However, the best time in my country is spring. Since the weather is mild and wet, all the flowers come out early and it's beautiful everywhere.

Why don't you come and see for yourself?

Model answer B

Do you have problems with the environment and pollution in your country?

Water is the big problem in my country, both too much water and too little! Let me explain.

I come from Spain, and like other European countries we have many problems with the environment. In the north, we have experienced heavy storms, with rainfall so heavy that whole campsites have been washed away. This water is very destructive, especially if the rivers get too full and break their banks. The authorities are trying to repair the banks, and to protect them, but it is very hard to do.

Then in the south of my country we have the opposite problem. Some areas have months and even years of drought. The farmers can't grow anything, and soon there won't be enough water for all the houses.

What can we do? There are plans to take salt water from the sea and turn it into fresh water, and another obvious answer is that we must find a way to get all the water in the north down to the south, where it is needed.

If you know a way to do it, please tell my government!

READING AND USE OF ENGLISH

Part 6

1. **A** Siberian tiger: Russia, China and North Korea
   B White rhino: Central and southern Africa
   C Humpback whale: They are found around the world (e.g. off the coasts of Canada, Iceland, Japan, Mexico, Caribbean), and they migrate up to 25,000 km a year.

2. **Possible answers**
   Whales eat fish, white rhinos eat grass and Siberian tigers eat other animals.
   Both whales and white rhinos tend to travel in groups but Siberian tigers live alone.
   Rhinos enjoy the hot sun whereas Siberian tigers live in colder climates.
   Rhinos live on grassland but Siberian tigers prefer woods and forests.
   Both whales and rhinos like water. Rhinos like to be in muddy pools, whereas whales swim in the ocean.

3. **Possible answers**
   They're beautiful, they attract tourists, people photograph them a lot, they're endangered (all three are rare animals that could become extinct. They are on the WWF Red List of endangered animals.).

4. C

Exam task

1 C 2 D 3 G 4 B 5 F 6 A

5 2 If you really can't answer one question when you have done all the others, guess!

3 The writer is comparing whales to humans and emphasising the importance of music to both. He or she wants his readers to identify with the whales, to empathise with them. He or she is trying to keep the reader's interest.

READING AND USE OF ENGLISH

Part 2

Grammar – Articles

1 1 *a or an* 2 the 3 the 4 no article 5 no article 6 the

2 *Oceans*, *seas* and *rivers*: the Amazon, the Atlantic Ocean, the Thames

Regions: the Far East, the north of England

Countries with the word *republic*, *kingdom*, *states*: the Czech Republic, the United Kingdom, the United States

Deserts and mountain ranges: the Himalayas, the Sahara

NB The following do not need *the* in front of them: California, Italy, Lake Como, London, South America

3 1 a; the 2 a; the 3 a; the 4 the; a 5 the

4 1 – 2 the 3 the 4 –

5 1 the 2 the 3 – 4 an 5 a 6 the 7 – 8 The 9 – 10 – 11 – 12 a 13 – 14 The 15 – 16 the 17 the 18 the 19 the 20 the

Grammar – *so* and *so/such* (*a/an*)

6 1 such 2 so 3 such 4 such 5 so 6 so

Rules: such; so

7 1 He hasn't got / doesn't have enough money.

2 The hill is too steep (for her).

3 There is too much food (for him).

4 The suitcase isn't big enough (for all the clothes / for all his things).

Exam task

1 only 2 ago 3 too 4 when 5 the 6 there 7 where 8 so

Unit 7

LISTENING

Part 3

1 A elegant, expensive-looking, formal, smart
   B individual, outrageous. second-hand, stylish, vintage
   C casual, comfortable, everyday

3

> **Recording script**
>
> I'm obsessed with keeping up with the latest trends. I like to stand out. I tend to wear outrageous clothes rather than more conventional ones. But they have to suit me and look really cool. As soon as something goes out of fashion, I stop wearing it. But I don't throw old clothes away as they sometimes come back into fashion. I know people who have loads of money and show off by wearing designer labels but I think you can look just as good in cheaper stuff.

4 1 be passionate about – be obsessed with
   2 staying in touch with – keeping up with
   3 look different – stand out
   4 slightly shocking – outrageous
   5 fairly typical – conventional
   6 look good on me – suit me
   7 becomes unfashionable – goes out of fashion
   8 get rid of – throw away
   9 become fashionable again – come back into fashion
   10 be very rich – have loads of money
   11 draw attention to yourself – show off
   12 clothes by particular designers – designer labels

Exam task

1 E 2 F 3 A 4 C 5 H

> **Recording script**
>
> *You will hear five people talking about shopping for clothes. For questions 1–5, choose from the list (A–H) what each speaker says. Use the letters only once. There are three extra letters which you do not need to use.*
>
> *Speaker 1*
>
> There isn't much to do round here at weekends, so I usually go to the shopping centre with my friends. We go in loads of shops and try stuff on, it's all too expensive for us but it's something to do. Most of it looks really bad on me as I'm really tall and thin but <u>I've got used to what kind of clothes look good on me</u> – things like long jumpers and skinny jeans. So when I've got some money, I know exactly what to look for. I like to have my friends with me though for a second opinion.

Speaker 2

Most of my friends want to get all the latest stuff but I never really know what to buy. So when I go to get something new, <u>I try to get what my mates are wearing</u>. Mostly we wear jeans and hoodies and, if we can afford them, designer T-shirts. They never really go out of fashion. I like going round the shops and looking at what's there but I'm not good at deciding and I'm not very adventurous with colours and styles. When I've got a lot of money, then I might decide to keep up with the latest fashions.

Speaker 3

My mum and my sister and I often go shopping together. We have a good time, especially if my mum is feeling generous, but she obviously likes different things from me. <u>She thinks I should wear bright cheerful things, whereas I like to wear grey or black.</u> She also thinks that being well-dressed is really important, so I should buy things that look smart and will last but I prefer to buy cheap clothes I can replace. I love going shopping with my best friend too. We've got completely different tastes but we like getting each other's opinions all the same.

Speaker 4

It annoys me that all the shops have the same things in them, then the fashion suddenly changes and one day everybody's wearing long shorts and then the next day the latest thing is tight black jeans. Some styles really suit some people but not others, so it doesn't really work. I usually go shopping on my own because I find most of the chain stores a bit boring and <u>I'm looking for stuff that will make me look different from my friends.</u> I do find it eventually – sometimes it's just an unusual colour but often I invent my own fashion. Some of it might look a bit strange but I don't mind.

Speaker 5

I've been interested in clothes since I was little, when I used to argue with my mum about what I would wear – I used to refuse to wear colours that didn't match and I'm still the same. I take ages to get ready in the morning because <u>I want to look stylish and elegant.</u> It's not because I want people to notice me but because I feel better about myself when I've taken a bit of time. My friends like to get dressed up in their best clothes when they go out but the rest of the time they just wear jeans and a T-shirt. That's not for me.

SPEAKING
Part 1
1

	Like	Dislike	Neither like nor dislike
Sofia	music, playing guitar, singing, skiing, beach	mountains in summer, long walks, looking at the views	
Daniel	watching football (Barcelona), history and geography	playing football and other sports	English, science

Recording script

Examiner: What do you like doing in your free time, Sofia?

Sofia: I'm really into music, so I spend a lot of time playing the guitar and I enjoy singing. I attempt to play some of the songs from my favourite bands and one day I hope to be in a band myself.

Examiner: Daniel, do you like sports?

Daniel: I'm mad about football, of course, like everyone who comes from Barcelona. I love going to see them when they play at home.

Examiner: And do you play any sports?

Daniel: I'm not very keen on playing football myself. I prefer to watch it. And I don't really like playing other sports very much either.

Examiner: Sofia, what do you like to do when you're on holiday?

Sofia: I live near the sea so we usually go to the mountains for holidays. I'm very keen on skiing. I love to spend time out on the snow. I first learnt when I was four years old, so I'm quite good at it now.

Examiner: What about summer holidays?

Sofia: I'm not that interested in going to the mountains in the summer. I can't bear going for long walks and looking at the views. I suppose it's because my parents made me do it when I was little. I prefer being at the beach.

Examiner: What's your favourite subject at school, Daniel?

Daniel: Well, English is OK but it's not my favourite. History and geography are what I enjoy most. I don't mind doing science but I'm not very good at the practical stuff – the experiments. I'd prefer to study things like the history of science. I want to study history at university. I'd like to be a history teacher one day.

2

Like (✓)	Dislike (✗)	Neither like nor dislike
I'm <u>really into</u> music.	I'm <u>not very keen on</u> playing football myself.	Well, English is OK but it's <u>not my favourite</u>.
I <u>enjoy</u> singing.	I <u>don't really like</u> playing other sports very much.	I <u>don't mind</u> doing science.
I'm <u>mad about</u> football, of course.	I'm <u>not that interested in</u> going to the mountains in the summer.	
I <u>love</u> going to see them.	I <u>can't bear</u> going for long walks.	
I'm <u>very keen on</u> skiing.		
History and geography are <u>what I enjoy most</u>.		

Verbs and expressions followed by to infinitive or -ing form

3 *to* infinitive: attempt, hope, want, would like, would prefer, agree (Ex 4)

   -ing form: can't bear, don't mind, enjoy, be interested in, be keen on, look forward to (Ex 4), suggest (Ex 4), imagine (Ex4)

   either *to* infinitive or *-ing* form: like, love, prefer

4 **1** to come **2** seeing **3** to see **4** to come **5** to go **6** going **7** living **8** to go **9** to buy **10** playing

6 He talks about the bottom two photos.

Advantages: lots of choice, compare prices, convenient, you can try clothes on, more fun

Disadvantages: quite traditional, not much for teenagers, can't try things on, wait for the post

Recording script

In both photos people are shopping. Mmm, let me see … In the first picture, someone's shopping on the Internet. Er … well … this has lots of advantages because there's loads to choose from and you can compare prices. It's also really convenient as you can do it at home. The second picture, on the other hand, shows people shopping in the main street, maybe in a small town. Let me think for a moment … The shops look quite traditional and maybe there isn't too much there for people of my age. The advantage is that you can see what you are buying and try clothes on, whereas you can't do that on the Internet and, er, you have to wait for your purchases to arrive in the post. Not everyone would agree but I think that we need both ways of shopping because sometimes it's fun just to go out into the town when you want something.

7 **1** Mmm, let me see
   2 Let me think for a moment
   3 Not everyone would agree but I think

WRITING

Part 2: Letter and email

1 and 2

Hi Lauren,

You asked me to tell you about a famous person I admire. Well, that's easy! (**1**) <u>Nobody could impress me</u> more than Nelson Mandela!

He is (**2**) <u>famous for being</u> the first black president of South Africa, and for being (**3**) <u>the man who</u> brought freedom to his people. (**4**) <u>Despite</u> spending 27 years in prison, he never got **discouraged**. He (**5**) <u>managed to</u> keep smiling, stay **optimistic** and be **cheerful**. He never, ever gave up. He was amazingly **confident** and (**6**) <u>as a result</u> of this belief in himself, he achieved the most amazing things.

(**7**) <u>Even though</u> he was fighting a very cruel system, he was always **patient**, **polite** and **thoughtful** to those around him. He was originally a lawyer, and (**8**) <u>even</u> some of the warders in the prison admired him.

There is (**9**) <u>one other quality which</u> I really like. If you look at the photos and videos of him, you can see he was always laughing and smiling. There are photos of him dancing and meeting famous singers and film stars when he was president. He loved life and music! He (**10**) <u>comes across as</u> such a great guy! I wish I had met him.

4 • *Openings*: Dear Lauren, Hi Lauren, Hello Lauren
   • *Endings*: I hope that's everything you wanted to know. / That's all I have time for now.
      Write to me again soon, / Best wishes, / Love

Remember that the letter is about giving information; there is no space in 140–190 words for 'chat'. The register in the main part of the letter is fairly formal, and that's the register you should use in your reply.

Exam task

Model answer 1

> Hello Andrew,
>
> You asked me to write and tell you about the person I admire most in my family. It's definitely my mother.
>
> She always manages to be cheerful, and she's very patient with my little brothers and me. She never gets discouraged, even when we do badly at school, and somehow she gets us organised so we can sort things out for ourselves. She's thoughtful too, so we always get birthday presents that we really like, and at weekends we have fun with her and Dad, just going to the beach near us, or having friends round.
>
> Mum has a job. She's a manager in the local supermarket, so she works hard. Despite having very little time for herself while we were young, she's done very well, and she got promotion quickly. I think she gives us a very good example of how you can be successful if you work hard and make the most of your time.
>
> As you can see, I'm lucky to have a mum like this, and my brothers think so too. I hope that answers your question.
>
> Best wishes
>
> Tim

Model answer 2

> Hi Julia,
>
> You wanted me to write and tell you about a student in my college that I admire. I'm not going to tell you about someone who is the cleverest person in the school, or the best at sport, or even the best looking.
>
> I'm going to tell you about Robbie, who comes to school every day in his wheelchair. I've known him since he was at primary school, and he has been in his chair for three years now.
>
> He's grown up knowing that this was how his life would turn out, and he just gets on with things. He's absolutely brilliant with computers – better than some of the teachers I think – and he's decided that he wants a career with a computer company. His attitude is so positive that I'm sure he will succeed. He's very artistic, and enjoys drawing. He's also very funny, and he tries not to take his problems too seriously.
>
> As a result, we all like him, and we look after him if he needs help.
>
> I hope that answers your question.
>
> Love
>
> Jo

READING AND USE OF ENGLISH
Part 5

1 annoyed, angry, furious, irritated (possibly upset)
2 C

Exam task

1 B 2 D 3 B 4 C 5 D 6 A

READING AND USE OF ENGLISH
Part 4

Grammar – Reported speech

1 1 was 2 seemed 3 was feeling 4 had lived 5 would have to 6 had been shopping (*was shopping* also possible) 7 had gone 8 had seen 9 was 10 cheer up 11 wanted 12 needed

2

Tense in direct speech	Tense in reported speech
present simple	past simple
present continuous	past continuous
present perfect simple	past perfect
will	would
past continuous	past perfect continuous
past simple	past perfect

3 The girl's mum asked her how she was.
The girl's mum asked if she wanted to go shopping. (We use *come* when we ask someone to join us in doing something but, when we report the sentence, *come* changes to *go*.)
We use *if* when we report a *yes/no* question.

4 1 why he was so late.
2 what she was watching.
3 if he had scored a goal.
4 if there was any food left.
5 when he would be home.
6 if she had seen his bag.

5 *The verbs which fit the gap are*: advised, asked, encouraged, persuaded, reminded, told, warned
The verbs which don't fit the gap are: agreed, explained, mentioned, said
Agree isn't followed directly by an object like *her*, and *said*, *explained* and *mentioned* would be followed by *to her*.

6 1 reminded 2 agreed 3 warned 4 mention

7 1 said 2 told 3 asked 4 told 5 told 6 asked 7 told them 8 asked

Exam task

1 it was picked up by
2 told her not to

3 Does anyone know how
4 such a long film
5 would have lent
6 us not to go

Unit 8

READING AND USE OF ENGLISH
Part 7
1 **Suggested answers**
   Photo 1 ecology/biology/geography – They are carrying out a survey/investigating wildlife, clean water, river flow, etc.
   Photo 2 maths/physics – They are doing calculations and solving equations.
   Photo 3 chemistry – They are measuring substances in test tubes.
2 *ecology*: ecosystems, endangered species, pollution, recycling
   biology: cells, diseases, ecosystems, endangered species, genetics, plants
   chemistry: gases, plastics
   physics: electricity, heat, light, mirrors, sound
   mathematics: fractions, geometry, percentages

Exam task
1 A 2 B 3 D 4 C 5 B 6 A 7 D 8 C 9 D 10 B

WRITING
Part 1: Essay
Grammar – Relative clauses
1 1 who 2 which 3 which 4 whose 5 which 6 who
2 1 You can omit the relative pronoun in 3 as it is not the subject of the verb which follows it ('other kids' is the subject of 'have covered'). In sentences 1 and 2 the relative pronoun is the subject of the verb which follows, so you can't omit the relative pronoun.
   2 You can put *that* in 1, 2 and 3, (all defining clauses). You cannot use *that* in non-defining clauses.
   3 A non-defining clause has commas around it, a defining clause does not.
3 1 which / that 2 whose 3 which / that / – 4 which / that / – 5 who 6 which 7 which 8 who / that
4 **A** doesn't fit. It contradicts what the student wrote in paragraphs 1 and 2.
   B fits well. It follows logically from what the student wrote in paragraphs 1 and 2, and uses an example from the student's own country, which is a good idea.
5 Paragraph 1: good for everyone to study science (important subject), good to study till 18 if *you like science and want a career in science*

Paragraph 2: *not good if you are weak in science; difficult for teachers / frustrating for bad students*
Paragraph 3: *system in own country; everyone studies till 16, then they can choose*
Conclusion: *everyone needs to study science, but till 18 is too long; 16 is better.*
Completed essay

> I certainly agree that all students should study science at school. It's a subject which is incredibly important in our world today. However, I think the issue of how long students should study it is more difficult. If you are the kind of student whose main interest is to become a doctor or a physicist, then certainly you will want to study science until you are 18. You will probably enjoy it too, because science is the subject that you are interested in, and probably the one which you are good at.
>
> But less able students, who find it difficult to pass exams in physics, biology and chemistry, will not be enthusiastic. These subjects, which can be hard at higher levels, may prove too challenging for them. The students will then get very frustrated with science, which means they will behave badly in class. That will make things very difficult for the teachers that are responsible for them.
>
> In my country, students study science until they are 16, and then choose whatever subjects they like until they are 18. I think this is a good system. I would therefore like to conclude by saying that I do not agree with the idea that all students should study science until the age of 18.

6 1 E 2 B 3 B 4 E 5 E 6 B
7 1 discovered 2 argue 3 claim 4 warned 5 say 6 think 7 encourage 8 disagree
8 1 Three
   2 Yes, the student talks about both the points given, then adds his own view (that governments need to act and spend money on the problem). He then reaches a clear conclusion; he is optimistic about the future and disagrees with the statement.
   3 Students' personal views.

Exam task

Model answer

Do you think in future it will be possible for robots to become doctors and teachers?

I certainly think that robots have a big part to play in the future of medicine. In many hospitals robots are already being used to perform operations, because they are far more accurate than human beings. However, robots do not work alone. Their 'hands' are used, but they are always controlled by human surgeons. Also, it's always human doctors and nurses who talk to the patients and deal with their worries.

As for robots being teachers, I think this is impossible. A teacher needs to communicate with students and encourage them, and a robot simply cannot do this. Robots might be able to help with simple tasks like marking homework, but they will never be able to replace teachers in the classroom because they cannot deal with pupils' questions or feelings.

I think these two examples give a clear answer to the question. In my personal opinion, humans will increasingly work with robots which will do the technical tasks. However, robots cannot work alone; they always need a human master.

I would like to conclude by saying that I am pleased about this. I would not like people to be replaced by machines.

READING AND USE OF ENGLISH

Part 3

Vocabulary – Computers

1 1 update / spreadsheet   2 3 log out   4 email   5 browser   6 webcam

2 1 drive   2 back   3 data   4 password   5 log   6 bookmark   7 installed   8 applications

Vocabulary – Word building (3)

3 application   attachment   automatically   easily   powerful

Verb	Noun	Adjective	Adverb
disable	*disability*	ABLE	*ably*
enable	*ability*	*unable*	
		disabled	
	COMMERCE	*commercial*	*commercially*
COMPETE	*competition*	*competitive*	*competitively*
	competitor	*uncompetitive*	*uncompetitively*

4 To make nouns, add *-ity, -tion, -or*
To make adjectives, add *-d, -al, -ive*

5 1 adverb   2 adjective   3 noun   4 noun   5 noun   6 noun   7 adverb   8 adjective   9 noun   10 adjective

6 2 technological   3 ability   4 popularity   5 weight   6 development   7 actually   8 unrecognisable   9 competition   10 powerful

7 *Unrecognisable* has the prefix; others which can be made negative are: *inability, unpopularity*

8 There is a rule for when we use *im-, ir-* and *il-*. Im- is usually used before words beginning with *p* and *m*, *ir-* is usually used before a word beginning with *r*, and *il-* before a word beginning with *l*. These are much less common than *un-, in-* or *dis-*.

disapproval   inexperienced   unfortunate   dishonesty
illegal   impatient   impolite   unreliable   irresponsible
dissatisfied   misunderstanding

Exam task

1 dramatic   2 Initially   3 permission   4 illegally   5 strength   6 passionate   7 knowledge   8 helpful

SPEAKING

Part 3

2 1 Yes   2 Yes   3 No   4 Yes

Recording script

Examiner: Now, I'd like you to talk about something together for about two minutes. I'd like you to talk about how important some inventions are in our daily lives. Here are some different inventions.
All right?

Karolina: Shall I begin?

Miguel: OK.

Karolina: Well, I use my laptop every day for my homework and for fun too – I watch films on it and listen to music.

Miguel: Yes, it's the same for me. But computers are also crucial for most people at work and for everything really. Nothing would work without computers.

Karolina: What about the fridge?

Miguel: Food wouldn't last so long without a fridge. But we could live without it I suppose – it's not so essential.

Karolina: And people would have to go shopping every day so they might waste less food. But they are vital in very hot countries, of course.

Miguel: Yeah, you're right. And we couldn't live without cars, could we? I can't wait to learn to drive. It's so annoying having to get the bus everywhere.

Karolina: Don't you think we ought to try to be less dependent on cars though?

Miguel:	That's not going to happen, is it? Lots of people like cycling but I don't think bicycles are a basic necessity in the same way as a car.
Karolina:	I agree, although I think in some countries they are more important as a way of travelling. Most people live in cities though, and cycling can be dangerous in traffic.
Miguel:	The last thing to talk about is a TV. What do you think about that?
Karolina:	Well, it's not so significant now because you can watch TV on your computer or even your phone.
Miguel:	But you can't sit down and watch a film with friends on a phone. It's too small!
Karolina:	That's true.
Miguel:	I would miss my TV. I like lying on the sofa in front of it when I'm tired.

3 1 One of the students starts the conversation with 'Shall I begin?'
   2 They say things like 'What about the ...?' 'The last thing to talk about is a ...'
   3 They say '..., don't you think?' 'What do you think about that?'
   4 'It's the same for me', 'You're right', 'I agree, although I think ...', 'That's true'.

4 **Suggested answers**
   serious, urgent, significant, crucial, vital, essential, a necessity

5 Computers are also **crucial** for most people at work.
   (A fridge) is not so **essential**
   (Fridges) are **vital** in very hot countries
   I don't think bicycles are **a basic necessity**
   (TV) isn't so **significant** now

6 Karolina thinks the TV and the laptop, and Miguel thinks the bicycle and the laptop. They don't agree on both things and it doesn't matter.

Recording script

Examiner:	Now you have a minute to decide which two inventions will become less important in the future.
Karolina:	Do you want to start?

Miguel:	Well, I think we've already said that the bicycle isn't as important in people's lives as the others, so I think that will definitely become less important.
Karolina:	It might not if we had special cycle lanes in towns. And if petrol gets too expensive and people get greener, they might all buy bicycles – even you!
Miguel:	I suppose so. Which would you choose then?
Karolina:	I think people will stop watching TV in their living rooms, so the traditional TV might disappear. I choose the TV and maybe the laptop because that's the same really – people can do everything on their phone or a tablet and they won't need a TV, a laptop and a phone as well.
Miguel:	Well, I still think the bicycle will be less important but I agree with you about the laptop. I think they're probably too big and heavy to carry about. So we don't quite agree.
Examiner:	OK. Don't worry. Thank you.

7 1 She asks Miguel: Do you want to start?
   2 Which would you choose then?
   3 I still think …

Part 4

Exam task

Possible answers

It's important in many subjects, and we use computers a lot. It's essential for science and media classes.

I like watching television occasionally. I particularly like films and comedy programmes.

No, definitely not. We communicate with technology, on our computers and mobile phones. It's just a different way of doing it.

It's not a bad thing that people are very dependent on mobile phones. I can't really imagine a world without them.

I think parents need to be careful what young children watch on TV, but some television is fun for them, and they can also learn a lot from it.

LISTENING

Part 1
1 C 2 E 3 H 4 F 5 B 6 G 7 A 8 D

Exam task
1 B 2 C 3 A 4 B 5 A 6 B 7 C 8 B

> **Recording script**
>
> *You will hear people talking in eight different situations.*
>
> *For questions 1–8, choose the best answer, A, B or C.*
>
> *Question One. You hear a brother and sister talking.*
>
> Boy: Hey sis, I've lost everything I wrote yesterday and I've no idea why. Fortunately I backed it up on my memory stick, so I won't have to start again. Have you had any trouble with the laptop today?
>
> Girl: Well, I know it's getting old, but it hasn't crashed on me or anything. I've been using it this morning and it seems OK. Hang on, is your project called 'Magnetism'?
>
> Boy: Yeah …
>
> Girl: Well, it's here, look, in my documents. You must have forgotten to switch user …
>
> Boy: OK.
>
> Girl: The Internet's slow though – I lost the connection once. I don't think broadband is very fast here in the village …
>
> *Question Two. You hear a sports programme on the radio.*
>
> Presenter: … and with another of the season's big races coming up tomorrow, conditions could be interesting … temperatures are set to fall rapidly overnight, with some mist forming. That may not clear completely by the time the race starts and that will mean some frost, so the track could be slippery. There were a few incidents during the last race today, with cars skidding and bumping into each other, so let's hope we don't get a repeat. Things will improve the day after, when sunny intervals and showers are predicted, so it will mean muddy conditions on the rugby field again at the weekend …

Question Three. You hear a teacher talking to his class.

Teacher: Well, I'm glad you've sorted out that little problem of leaving litter on the sports field, and just in time because we're holding a major hockey competition here on Saturday for all the schools in the area. We'd appreciate some help with that. We need about 20 volunteers, some in the car park to show where parents can drop players off, some indoors making sure everyone knows where the changing rooms are, and a few more to assist with refreshments half-way through the competition. I'll pass a list round. Put a tick against your name if you're willing to help …

Question Four. You hear a boy and girl talking about school.

Boy: You know I've always hated maths, Lucy, but I've done much better since we've had that new teacher. He makes it all seem logical …

Girl: Mmm, for me maths is relaxing – it's all there on the page. I don't enjoy the classes with the new teacher though. Although he is really good at explaining, he goes too far and makes it all a bit too simple. I'm not being pushed hard at all, you know, asked to do really difficult things in algebra and geometry and so on.

Boy: Well, yeah. If the class is right for me, it's not going to be right for you, is it?

Girl: I don't know about that …

Question Five. You hear a boy talking to his sister about a shopping trip.

Girl: How was the shopping trip, then?

Boy: The new computer store is great. You can't get near any of the play stations and stuff because there are so many people, but they sell some great games.

Girl: Where else did you go?

Boy: That fast food place. I lost Joe and Mike on the way there. I thought they were just playing a trick on me when they didn't reply to my texts. So <u>I hid behind one of the little trees outside the fast food place and gave them a real shock when they walked past! I wish I hadn't done it now; they were upset because they couldn't find me.</u>

Girl: Oh, are you still speaking?

Boy: Just about …

Question Six. You hear a girl talking to her class about her visit to an aquarium.

Girl: Well yeah, I thought this visit was cool. I've done so many school trips to museums and there's only so many glass cases you can look at, even if you're interested in history! The exhibits here were alive. You walked through the glass tunnels in the aquarium and you could see the fish swimming just above your head. <u>And then there was a place where you could actually touch some weird flat fish called rays, which really made the visit for me.</u> Everyone should have a go at that if they can. There was a café which had an exhibition of lovely paintings and photos, too. They looked like the real thing I'd just seen.

Question Seven. You hear a boy talking about a cookery competition he entered.

Boy: … my catering teacher encouraged me to enter a baking competition, and I decided to make a cheesecake. You need lots of ingredients: biscuits and butter for the base, soft cheese, eggs, vanilla, sugar and cream for the filling and fresh raspberries and lemon for the sauce. I knew it was important not to forget anything. <u>I could have played safe and made something very straightforward, but I wanted to make something that would impress.</u> I was nervous – there were lots of competitors – and I forgot to put the cream into the filling. The cheesecake was great though – very firm. And the judges loved it – I came second. Result!

Question Eight. You hear a father and daughter talking about a holiday.

Girl: The holiday centre in Holland sounds great, Dad, but why are we hiring bikes?

Father: Well, <u>the idea is that once you've arrived and put your luggage into the cabins, you park your vehicle and leave it.</u> I think it's a good system. but I'm wondering about getting the train there once we've taken the ferry to Holland. There's a station near the holiday centre. And actually there's a direct coach … we could take that from the port …

Girl: Yeah, Dad, but we'll want to get out and about, won't we? Not spend all our time in the centre …

Father: Yep, you're right. We'll stick to my original idea.

Girl: Good.

REVISION EXERCISES ANSWER KEY

Units 1 and 2

1 1 arrive   2 're camping   3 don't understand   4 'll be sitting
   5 don't recognise   6 'm doing   7 hear   8 come

2 1 are not /aren't as / so wide as
   2 far more noise
   3 is much longer than / takes much more time than
   4 like best is not / isn't far
   5 less often than

3 1 C   2 B   3 D   4 A   5 B   6 C   7 A   8 D

4 1 will be   2 I arrive   3 arrives   4 I think   5 it will take
   6 I've done   7 I'll come   8 I'm looking forward   9 I know
   10 I'm staying   11 like   12 will be   13 I've never seen
   14 Is there   15 you live

5 1 d was playing   2 f had already gone   3 h came
   4 b haven't / have not managed   5 a didn't answer / did not answer   6 g haven't/have not eaten   7 c phoned
   8 e had seen

6 1 goes   2 're / are   3 'll / will be / 'm / am going to be
   4 'll / will let   5 invited   6 had never sailed   7 set
   8 was shining   9 've / have been having OR 've / have had
   10 knew

7 1 excitedly   2 definitely   3 easily   4 immediately
   5 usually   6 carefully   7 simply   8 particularly

8 1 mysterious   2 suitable   3 adventurous   4 reliable
   5 natural   6 furious   7 predictable   8 central

Units 3 and 4

1 1 While   2 Although   3 Even though   4 Although
   5 In spite of   6 Even though   7 Despite   8 Although

2 1 was cancelled   2 am being sent   3 has been played by
   4 had been advised (by my teacher)   5 will be taken
   6 is being made   7 were borrowed   8 is being put

3 1 sound technician   2 stuntman/woman   3 make-up artist
   4 producer   5 cameraman/woman   6 director
   7 costume designer   8 set decorator

4 1 science fiction   2 comedy   3 thriller   4 documentary
   5 western   6 cartoon   7 animation   8 horror   9 action film
   10 romantic comedy

5 1 three of violin, cello, piano, guitar   2 clarinet, saxophone, flute   3 five of pop, heavy metal, classical, punk, salsa, hip-hop, rock and roll, jazz, rap, soul   4 band   5 lyrics   6 tune
   7 album   8 fans

6 1 B   2 A   3 B   4 C   5 B   6 A   7 C   8 B

7 1 of   2 for   3 to   4 in   5 on   6 about   7 with   8 about
   9 of   10 about

8 1 pitch   2 referee   3 goalkeeper's   4 defenders   5 tackle
   6 umpire   7 serve   8 opponent   9 point   10 net

9 1 convenience   2 equality   3 generous   4 independence
   5 patient   6 conclusion   7 connection   8 divide
   9 expansion   10 persuade

Units 5 and 6

1. 1 i had been 2 g would have missed 3 e is 4 j need
   5 b help 6 h sets 7 c go 8 d would be 9 a started
   10 f don't / do not get
2. 1 secondary 2 majority 3 examination 4 comprehensive
   5 ability 6 challenging 7 variety 8 possibility 9 choice
   10 application(s)
3. 1 a 2 – 3 – 4 the 5 the 6 – 7 the 8 – 9 The 10 a
   11 the 12 – / the 13 – 14 the 15 – / the 16 the 17 a
   18 – 19 the 20 an
4. 1 such beautiful roses 2 so exciting 3 such good memories
   4 so good 5 such a marvellous evening 6 such a tasty
   risotto 7 so important 8 such a good laugh 9 so beautiful
   as 10 such a perfect volleyball team
5. 1 air conditioning 2 electrical equipment 3 email
   attachment 4 fresh ingredients 5 local produce 6 plastic
   bags 7 ready meals 8 recycled paper 9 reduce waste
   10 take a shower
6. 1 reduce waste 2 take a shower 3 electrical equipment
   4 recycled paper 5 email attachment 6 air conditioning
   7 plastic bags 8 local produce 9 fresh ingredients
   10 ready meals
7. 1 sympathetic 2 competitive 3 decisive 4 communicative
   5 creative 6 determined 7 cheerful 8 energetic
8. 1 would rather 2 is looking forward 3 would like
   4 can't imagine 5 would prefer 6 dislike 7 have never
   been able 8 suggested

Units 7 and 8

1. 1 to go 2 to fall 3 to do 4 taking 5 swimming
   6 relaxing 7 driving 8 to find 9 putting 10 go
   11 looking 12 to go
2. 1 explained (that) he couldn't
   2 agreed to help / agreed (that) she would help
   3 so I can't come
   4 hadn't seen such a
   5 told me she liked
   6 if I knew
3. 1 dress 2 suit 3 make 4 get 5 look 6 keep 7 show
   8 go 9 come 10 try 11 have 12 get
4. 1 passionate 2 frustrated 3 optimistic 4 curious 5 guilty
   6 patient
5. ashamed 5 confident 3 enthusiastic 1 furious 2
   interested 4 irritated 2
6. 1 who 2 whose 3 which / that 4 who / that 5 where
   6 where 7 which 8 which / that / –
7. 1 recycling 2 disease 3 endangered 4 cell
   5 conservation 6 genetics 7 atom 8 electricity
8. 1 strength 2 powerful 3 originally 4 possibilities
   5 impolite 6 attractive 7 commercials 8 misunderstanding

WRITING GUIDE ANSWER KEY

Writing Part 1

Essay

1. 1 your English teacher
   2 yes
   3 no, it's not necessary
   4 yes
2. Paragraphs 1,2 and 4 discuss **point 1**, which subjects are most useful. Paragraph 3 talks about **point 2**: which are easier. The candidate says that science subjects are only useful for certain jobs, whereas languages are useful for everyone, and that science subjects are very difficult for many people.
   The candidate's **third point** (in paragraph three) is that people should study both science and languages if possible.
   The conclusion is that everyone should study foreign languages.

Plan:
Paragraph 1: 'which is more useful' depends on what job you are doing/science isn't useful for everyone
Paragraph 2: learning different languages is useful for everyone
Paragraph 3: Good to study both sciences and languages if possible, but science more difficult
Paragraph 4: everyone should study languages

Linking phrases:
<u>I would like to start my essay by saying that</u> whether languages or sciences are more useful depends very much on what job you would like to do. If you want to be a doctor, or a great inventor, <u>of course</u> you will need to study science subjects. <u>However, I would argue that</u> there really isn't much point in studying science subjects <u>if</u> you are going to be a history teacher, or work in a shop.

<u>On the other hand,</u> learning languages is always useful, whatever career you want to have in the future. <u>Of course,</u> English is very useful <u>because</u> so many people speak it, <u>but</u> other languages, like Spanish and Chinese, are <u>also</u> very important.

<u>I think that it is good to study both</u> sciences <u>and</u> languages <u>if</u> you can, <u>but</u> not many people will become experts in science. <u>That is because</u> for most people, science beyond a certain level is far too difficult, <u>although</u> it's good to have a basic knowledge.

<u>Therefore, I would like to conclude by saying that</u>, ideally, everyone should study several foreign languages, <u>simply because</u> they are useful in every job.

Writing Part 2

Story

1. 1 teacher/other students who read the school website
   2 a day

3 The events don't have to be positive. They weren't planned. The story begins *I was expecting to have a quiet day, but it turned out to be just the opposite.*

2. The **first point** is in the second paragraph: *George told me there was a robbery going on.*
   The **second point** is in the first paragraph: *...when the phone rang.*

Past tenses
Simple past is used throughout: *turned out, was, asked, rushed, told, said, phoned, arrived, took, were, appeared*
Past continuous: *was expecting, was reading, were being removed (passive)*
Past perfect: *had driven up, had stopped*
Past perfect continuous: *had been moving*
The **direct speech** is used by the candidate/narrator to his friend George. It adds excitement and tension to the story, and shows how the boys are feeling.
Effective vocabulary and expressions: reading sleepily, there's a much simpler explanation, said impatiently, arrived very rapidly, our picture appeared in the paper
The title sets the scene for the story and makes you want to read on. The candidate has clearly planned what he/she is going to write about. So always give your story a title!

Review

1. 1 other teenagers
   2 in a magazine
   3 Any kind – as long as you really like it yourself.
   4 You don't have to recommend it – the question says '*whether* you would recommend it to other people'. However, if it's your favourite website, and you spend a lot of time on it, you will probably recommend it to someone!
2. **Linking words and phrases:** see underlining below
   Verb tenses: The main tense used is the present simple. Other tenses are:
   Present perfect: *have been*
   Present continuous: *I'm learning*
   Future: *you will find*

The best website I <u>have been</u> on is ultimateguitar.com. I spend lots of time on it <u>because I'm learning</u> to play the electric guitar and everything I need is on this site.

It has reviews of all kinds of guitar music, <u>which means</u> jazz and classical <u>as well as</u> pop, rock and so on, <u>so</u> there is something for different tastes. <u>In addition</u>, there is always news and gossip about well-known guitarists. <u>And better still,</u> there are really good interviews to watch, with rock stars, classical guitarists and so on.

<u>However</u>, the most fantastic thing about the site is that you can download tabs for all your favourite guitar music from it. It has all the famous riffs and they add new music every week. <u>It's such a</u> popular feature <u>that</u> there is sometimes a queue for

downloading. I set it up before school, <u>so</u> it's there when I get home.

I love this website, and I would recommend it to other guitar fans, <u>especially if</u> they are players themselves. And <u>even if you don't</u> play, I'm sure <u>you will find</u> it interesting!

Vocabulary:
Websites: *site, to go on a website, download, tabs*
Music: *electric guitar, jazz, classical, pop, rock, rock stars, (classical)guitarist, tabs, riffs, players*

Letter and email

1 1 your English friend Hannah
   2 You can write about a city anywhere in the world, but it must be a **capital** city.
   3 Yes. You're asked to recommend something for a tourist to visit – that could be anything, including cafes, shops, a funfair, a sports stadium, etc.

2 Historical facts: *Romans, French kings, Baron Haussmann, French Revolution,*
Places to visit: *The Louvre, the Latin Quarter, the River Seine*
Friendly phrases: *Your history project sounds fascinating!, Best wishes*

3 Thanking, Stating opinion or preference, Suggesting and recommending, Giving reasons, Apologising, Making requests and offers, Asking questions.

Article

1 1 in a teenage magazine
   2 teenagers of different nationalities
   3 No, you don't have to use the suggestions, but you can if you wish.

2 Plan:
Paragraph 1: Moon always important / beauty
Paragraph 2: Space travel/living on the moon / science fiction
Paragraph 3: Children's stories/songs/poems

Set text

1 Miss Havisham
Appearance: still dressed for her wedding; her dress has turned yellow
Behaviour: she stopped all the clocks in the house and lives in the past; because of what happened to her, she brought Estelle up to dislike men
She is strange because her future husband stood her up on her wedding day, and she has never got over the shock.

2 Phantom of the Opera: Plan
Paragraph 1: explain who phantom was – Erik, a man with an ugly face who lived in the Opera house, a real person, not a ghost, loved Christine
Paragraph 2: sad life, poor, made to wear a mask
Paragraph 3: Erik travelled, was brilliant, built Opera house for Christine
Relevant parts of the plot: normal person, not a ghost, built Opera House, taught Christine to sing and fell in love with her, born in a poor village, made to wear a mask

Acknowledgements

Author acknowledgements
The authors would like to thank their editors: Louise Wood, Alyson Maskell, Diane Hall and Ann-Marie Murphy for their expertise and support. Many thanks also to Matt Stephens (production project manager), Chloe Szebrat (assistant permissions clearance controller), Louise Edgeworth (freelance picture researcher), Leon Chambers (audio producer) and Sue Flood (proof reader). Many thanks also go to Tracey and the team at Wild Apple.

Publisher acknowledgements
The authors and publishers are grateful to the following for reviewing the material during the writing process:

Susan Obiglio: Argentina; Maria Christaki: Greece; Jane Hoatson, Jessica Smith, Catherine Toomey: Italy; Katherine Bilsborough, Laura Clyde: Spain; Ludmila Kozhevnikova: Russia; Bridget Bloom, Helen Chilton, Mark Fountain, Rebecca Raynes: UK.

Thanks are also due to the teachers who contributed to the initial research into this course. In Italy: Judith Axelbury, Liane Hyde, Rachel Shields, Prof. Barbagallo, Prof. Marrali, Prof. Cook, Prof. Dickens, Prof. Grasso, Prof. Zoppas, Prof. Lovati, Prof. Risso. In Poland: teachers at Empik, Warsaw Study Centre, Warsaw University and ZS UMK. In Spain: Keith Appleby, Vicante Ferarios Maroto, Nick Tunstall, and Lisa Wotton. In Switzerland: Keith Dabourn, Ms Eigner, Amy Jost, Ueli Hepp, Lori Kaithen, Eveline Reichel, Lee Walker, teachers at Berlitz, Berufschule Bulach, Sprachschule Schneiner and Liz and Michelle from the apprenticeship school.

Development of this publication has made use of the Cambridge English Corpus (CEC). The CEC is a computer database of contemporary spoken and written English, which currently stands at over one billion words. It includes British English, American English and other varieties of English. It also includes the Cambridge Learner Corpus, developed in collaboration with the University of Cambridge ESOL Examinations. Cambridge University Press has built up the CEC to provide evidence about language use that helps to produce better language teaching materials.

This product is informed by the English Vocabulary Profile, built as part of English Profile, a collaborative programme designed to enhance the learning, teaching and assessment of English worldwide. Its main funding partners are Cambridge University Press and Cambridge ESOL and its aim is to create a 'profile' for English linked to the Common European Framework of Reference for Languages (CEFR). English Profile outcomes, such as the English Vocabulary Profile, will provide detailed information about the language that learners can be expected to demonstrate at each CEFR level, offering a clear benchmark for learners' proficiency. For more information, please visit www.englishprofile.org

Text acknowledgements
The authors and publishers acknowledge the following sources of copyright material and are grateful for the permissions granted. While every effort has been made, it has not always been possible to identify the sources of all the material used, or to trace all copyright holders. If any omissions are brought to our notice, we will be happy to include the appropriate acknowledgements on reprinting.

Robin's Nest Productions, Inc for the text on p. 10 adapted from *Hold on Tight* by Robin Gunn, Copyright © 1998 Robin Gunn. Reproduced with permission; DOGO Media, Inc for the text on p. 51 adapted from 'Even Humpback Whales release hit singles' by Meera Dolasia, DOGONews, 15/4/2011. Reproduced with permission; Random House Group Limited for the text on pp. 58-9 adapted from *The Tarot Reader's Daughter* by Helen Dunwoodie, published by Corgi Books. Reprinted by permission of The Random House Group Ltd;

Photo Acknowledgements
The authors and publishers acknowledge the following sources of copyright material and are grateful for the permissions granted. While every effort has been made, it has not always been possible to identify the sources of all the material used, or to trace all copyright holders. If any omissions are brought to our notice, we will be happy to include the appropriate acknowledgements on reprinting.

p. 6 (A): Alamy/©Steve Skjold; p. 6 (B): Getty Images/Lonely Planet Images/©Michael Coyne; p. 6 (C): Thinkstock/Big Cheese Photo; p. 7: Getty Images/Lonely Planet Images/©Christer Fredriksson; p. 8 (L): Alamy/© European Sports Photographic Agency; p. 8 (R): Corbis/© Tetra Images; p. 9 (TL): Thinkstock/David De Lossy; p. 9 (TC): Fotolia/©Mr Markin; p. 9 (TR): istockphoto/©Alija; p. 9 (BR): Thorpe Park; p. 12: www.CartoonStock.com; p. 14 (L): Fotolia/©Gail Johnson; p. 14 (C): Fotolia/© MikIG; p. 14 (R): Alamy/©Stuart Pearce; p. 17: Fotolia/©erika palla; p. 18 (L): Alamy/©David L Moore; p. 18 (R): Alamy/©Image Source Plus; p. 19 (L): Alamy/© Elizabeth Czitronyi; p. 19 (C): Superstock/©imagebroker.net; p. 19 (R): Alamy/©Peter Phipp/Travelshots.com; p. 22: Fotolia/©Miravision; p. 23 (T): The Kobal Collection/Lucasfilm/Paramount Pictures; p. 23 (AC): Rex Features/©Sony Pics/Everett; p. 23 (BC): The Kobal Collection/Warner Bros/DC Comics; p. 23 (B): Alamy/©AF Archive; p. 24 (T): The Kobal Collection/Paramount Pictures; p. 24 (B): The Kobal Collection/Scren Gems; p. 26 (A): Glowimages/©Radius; p. 26 (B): Glowimages/©Stockbroker; p. 26 (C): Alamy/©Geoff du Feu; p. 26 (D): Corbis/©Redchopsticks; p. 27 (L): Getty Images/©Nick Onken; p. 27 (R): Superstock/©Eye Ubiquitous; p. 28: Alamy/©Hemis; p. 30 (L): Alamy/©Images-USA; p. 30 (R): Corbis/©Joachim Ladefoged/VII; p. 32 (T): Thinkstock/istockphoto; p. 32 (B): Getty Images/©Robert Decelis ltd; p. 33 (L): Alamy/©Darek Miszkiel; p. 33 (C): Getty Images/The Image Bank/©Jetta Productions; p. 33 (R): Corbis/©Piyal Adhikary/epa; p. 34: Glowimages/©Image Souce; p. 35: Masterfile; p. 36: www.CartoonStock.com; p. 38 (A): Alamy/©William Manning; p. 38 (B): Glowimages/©Cultura; p. 38 (C): Thinkstock/Digital Vision; p. 38 (D): Getty Images/©DreamPictures; p. 39 (A): Thinkstock/Comstock Images; p. 39 (B): Masterfile/©Aflo Relax; p. 39 (C): Alamy/©RubberBall; p. 39 (D): Corbis/©David Katzenstein/Citizenstock; p. 42 (A): Alamy/©Jon Parker Lee; p. 42 (B): Alamy/©Creative Collection Tolbert; p. 42 (C): Alamy/©Archimage; p. 42 (D): Alamy/©Aardvark; p. 42 (E): SuperStock/©View Pictures Ltd; p. 43: Aeroseum, Sweden; p. 44 (1): Corbis/©moodboard; p. 44 (2): Alamy/©MBI; p. 44 (3): Alamy/©El Chapulin; p. 44 (4): Alamy/©Chris Cooper-Smith; p. 46 (A): Superstock/©Minden Pictures; p. 46 (B): Alamy/©Philip Mugridge; p. 46 (C): Superstock/©Michael Wheatley/All Canada Photos; p. 46 (D): Alamy/©Greatstock Photographic Library; p. 48 (T): Corbis/©KidStock/Blend Images; p. 48 (B): Alamy/©Jeff Greenberg 3 of 6; p. 50 (A): Glowimages/©Wolfgang Kaehler; p. 50 (B): Shutterstock/©Stu Porter; p. 50 (C): istockphoto/©Jim Parkin; p. 54 (A): Alamy/©RubberBall; p. 54 (B): Alamy/©dov makabaw; p. 54 (C): Alamy/©John Powell-Photographer; p. 56 (T): Corbis/©Roberto Herrett/Loop Images; p. 54 (AC): Alamy/©Robert Stainforth; p. 56 (BC): Alamy/©David J Green - Lifestyle themes; p. 56 (B): Superstock/©ICP/age footstock; p. 62 (1): Alamy/©Martin Shields; p. 62 (2): Masterfile; p. 62 (3): Fotolia/©auremar; p. 63 (A): Masterfile/©Rick Gomez; p. 63 (B): Alamy/©Catchlight Visual Services; p. 63 (C): Thinkstock/iStock; p. 63 (D): Glowimages/©GogoImages; p. 65: Alamy/©WILDLIFE GmbH; p. 67: Rex Features/©Geoffrey Robinson; p. 68 (L): Thinkstock/iStock/Oleksiy Mark; p. 68 (R): Thinkstock/iStock/Mile Atanasov; p. 71: Corbis/©Ocean; p. 74: Alamy/©AfriPics.com; p. 77: Science Photo Library/©Emilio Segre Visual Archives/American Institute of Physics; p. 80: Corbis/©Joe Stevens/Retna Ltd; p. 90: Alamy/©Picture Press.

Illustrations by:
John Batten (Beehive Illustrations) pp. 20, 27; Maxwell Dorsey (NB Illustration) pp. 52, 53, 79, 80, 82, 85, 87; Richard Jones (Beehive Illustrations) pp. 10, 11, 15, 40; Kate Rochester (Pickled Ink Ltd) pp. 16, 25, 30, 35, 72; Laszlo Veres (Beehive Illustrations) pp. 22, 53, 58, 60